REA

W9-BNZ-763

THE PRACTICAL GUIDE TO QUALITY
CHILD CARE CENTERS

Dedication

To Carol Davis
with thanks for her moral support and her enthusiasm.

PS

To Fred Dyke
for his encouragement and support.

PCD

The
Practical Guide
to
Quality
Child Care

Pam Schiller and
Patricia Carter Dyke

gryphon House
Beltsville, MD

Preface

The purpose of this manual is to provide practical help to directors of child care centers. The ultimate goal is to improve the quality of programs for young children and, at the same time, help directors and teachers be more effective in their work.

Copyright

© 2001 Pam Schiller and Patricia Carter Dyke

Published by Gryphon House, Inc. 10726 Tucker Street, Beltsville, MD 20705 or

P.O. Box, Beltsville, MD 20705-0207

Visit us on the web at www.gryphonhouse.com

Library of Congress Cataloging-in-Publication Data

Schiller, Pamela Byrne.

   The practical guide to quality child care / Pam Schiller and Patricia Carter Dyke.

      p. cm.

   Includes bibliographical references and index.

   ISBN 0-87659-262-0

   1. Day care centers--Administration. I. Dyke, Patricia. II. Title.

HQ778.5 .S35 2001

362.71'2'068--dc21

                                                          2001035294

Photographs: Subjects & Predicates, Nancy P. Alexander

Disclaimer

The publisher and the authors cannot be held responsible for injury, mishap, or damages incurred during the use of or because of the information in this book.

Bulk purchase

Gryphon House books are available for special premiums and sales promotions as well as for fund-raising use. Special editions or book excerpts also can be created to specification. For details, contact the Director of Sales at the address above.

Table of Contents

Qualities and Characteristics of an Effective Director

1

The successful director of a child care center needs to be highly proficient in a wide range of skills. The responsibilities of child care directors include public relations, personnel management, time management, decision making, finance, and early childhood education (see the chart on page 17). In other business structures, designated individuals often handle each of these responsibilities and have been trained for their unique positions. However, this is not likely to be the case in the world of child care. Therefore, it is important for you as a director to evaluate your strengths and weaknesses in each of these areas in order to plan a realistic program that will enable you to meet your goals.

Subjects & Predicates

Profile of a Child Care Director

Child care directors must be able to work with staff, families, and children. Staff management, which is crucial to the success of a program, depends on your ability to communicate, motivate, delegate, and relate to people in a meaningful way. Working with families requires additional skills in audience sensitivity and public relations. Finally, children are the nucleus of a center. This necessitates an understanding of child development and a commitment to the work of the human services profession. Add a high tolerance for stress, and the profile of a child care director begins to emerge. The characteristics that are essential for an effective director, outlined below and on the chart on page 17, are defined in relation to the child care profession.

Characteristics of an Effective Director

- *Commitment* is the desire to have a positive impact on the lives of others. A director with commitment wants to make a difference in the lives of children, families, and staff.

- *Delegation* is the ability to see the strengths and interests of individual staff members and assign tasks so that each staff member grows and feels successful. Directors can enhance it when they look for the positive characteristics of staff.

- *Motivation* is reflected in a director's ability to stimulate the performance of staff by being creative, divergent, and enthusiastic. A director who motivates tends to put people into patterns that work toward the benefit of the whole program.

- *Relating to others* is defined as a director's ability to really know staff, families, and children. It requires a commitment to mutual support as well as an awareness of the possibility that not all staff will be successful.

- *Understanding children* means being aware of child development, which results in the ability to plan curriculum appropriate to children's needs. Directors utilize this knowledge to help educate families and staff to work effectively with children.

- *Understanding self* refers to a director's concept of his or her own values, attitudes, strengths, weaknesses, and goals. To direct others, a person must have a strong sense of self.

Orchestrating these skills and characteristics into effective job performance is the key to success. It takes time to perfect these skills, but each day provides opportunities for practice.

Determining Your Strengths and Opportunities for Growth

The self-evaluation instrument "Inventory of Director's Managerial Skills" (page 18) will help you determine your areas of strength and areas in which you have room to grow. Use this instrument for your own development, as well as for staff in-service training.

After you rate yourself on each statement, refer to the key at the bottom of the inventory to determine how the statements correlate with the characteristics described on the previous page. To determine a score for each characteristic, add the numerical values for the statements listed in each category. For example, suppose you answered the questions in the Commitment category as follows:

Statement 1: strongly agree (5)

Statement 8: neutral (3)

Statement 9: agree (4)

Statement 23: agree (4)

Statement 25: strongly agree (5)

Add the numerical values of each statement to get a total of 21. Now, divide 21 by the number of statements (5), and you arrive at an average of 4.2. According to the scale on the form "Inventory of Director's Managerial Skills," this indicates an area of strength. On the other hand, suppose that in the category Understanding Children (statements 5, 10, 13, and 17), you rated yourself 2, 3, 1, and 2. After adding these numbers and dividing by 4, you arrive at a score of 2. This indicates an area that needs improvement.

After you inventory your skills, you will have an idea of your strengths as well as the areas in which you need to improve. To plan for improvement, look closely at each statement in a category where your score indicates a need for improvement.

Continuing with the previous example, statement 5 indicates how well you know the children in the center and how sensitive you are to their individual needs. If you scored a 2 on this statement, it indicates definite room for improvement. It is important to improve on this characteristic so that you are informed when working with families and staff and in planning curricula.

Your first step toward improvement might be scheduling time each day to visit classrooms. You might also decide to review information in the children's files and perhaps even meet with teachers to discuss special needs of specific students. Getting to know the children is best handled by taking the time to "mingle."

You might also decide to enroll in child development classes at a local college or university. Many colleges offer child development course work as a part of continuing education programs. Visit a college bookstore to find books on child development (see Recommended Reading at the end of this chapter) and check the Internet (see Appendix F, Internet Resources, page 177). Both will prove to be sources of easily accessible information.

Statement 10 of the self-evaluation form on page 18 states, "I stay abreast of child development news information." In the previous example, your response to this statement indicated uncertainty. If this is the case, you might ask yourself the following questions:
~ When was the last time I attended a child development conference or workshop?
~ Do I hold memberships in professional organizations that are concerned with the education and care of young children?
~ Do I read child development journals and magazines?
~ Do I watch television specials that focus on young children?

If you answered yes to the above questions, you should have rated yourself higher. If you answered no, however, you need to get busy "catching up" and doing these things. You can get necessary information by contacting local universities or community colleges, libraries, or by writing or calling the National Association for the Education of Young Children (see Appendix F, Organizations, page 180).

Statement 13 of the self-evaluation form, "I help families understand curriculum." Again, in the example, your rating indicated that you do not do this. Therefore, you need to explore ways to inform families.

You might start by calling a staff meeting and brainstorming some possibilities. In addition, you might even survey families to ask what information would be helpful to them. Consider putting out a newsletter similar to the example in Appendix A (see page 109 or 113). Perhaps the center staff may want to schedule family conferences or even a family education seminar.

The last statement in the category, number 17, states, "I help families understand the behavior of their children." In the example, you rated yourself low. The suggestions for improvements mentioned in the previous statements might automatically promote improvement in this area. As you begin to know individual children better and to consult with their teachers, you will become better prepared to share information with their families. As you increase your child development knowledge through professional organizations, workshops, and publications, you will become familiar with solutions and strategies in child rearing. As you work with families to help them understand curriculum, you will also increase their understanding of behavior.

Change takes time. New approaches can't be implemented overnight. Although improving your weaker areas is a gradual process, each small step improves the overall product—you. A director needs a high level of self-esteem, a desire to learn from experience, the ability to function well with others, and an understanding of how to set and achieve goals. Take every opportunity to learn more about yourself and how you work. How well your center runs correlates directly with your self-understanding.

Suggestions for Growth

Let's look at a few suggestions for becoming more skilled in each of the five areas that represent the characteristics of an effective director.

Commitment is the desire to have a positive impact on the lives of others. A director with commitment wants to make a difference in the lives of children, families, and staff.

- Attend early childhood professional meetings. Make friends. Find people who have the same goals as you.
- Stay focused on your goals by verbally stating them to yourself each day as you arrive at work. People are more like to stay committed to what they stay focused on.
- Remind yourself often that you are making strides in your commitment to provide quality services to children and their families. Even small steps keep you moving forward.
- Demonstrate your commitment in all that you do. Stick to your goals. Endure setbacks with determination. Your actions speak louder than your words. Staff and families are watching and commitment is contagious. If others catch it, it will be easier for you to hold on to.
- Develop computer literacy. It is the way of today, not tomorrow. The computer is an important tool in any business. In addition to the obvious use of a word processing software program, the Internet provides resources on every aspect of the child care profession.

Delegation is the ability to see the strengths and interests of individual staff members and assign tasks so that each staff member grows and feels successful. It is enhanced when a director looks for the positive characteristics of staff.

- Practice delegating. Think of it like a puzzle that goes together in many different ways. It offers everyone a break when they try something new.
- Evaluate your staff to get to know their strengths, areas of growth potential, and learning styles. Think creatively for ways to enhance each individual's strengths.
- Encourage your staff to evaluate their own work Ask each staff member to complete the worksheet on page 18. It is helpful to know what they see as their strengths—you may learn something new.

- Experiment with letting staff members try out different tasks. You may find that the cook has a knack for creating bulletin boards or that the toddler teacher is really organized when it comes to planning a special event. Be sure you give authority to the person who is carrying out the assignment.
- Explain clearly the work that must be done, along with a deadline for each segment of the project. Ask the staff to complete their work before the deadline so that if there is a need for any adjustments, the time frame doesn't cause stress.
- The more you work at this, the better you get.
- Celebrate staff successes in new areas and their clever insights.

Motivation is reflected in the director's ability to stimulate the performance of staff by being creative, divergent, and enthusiastic. A person who motivates tends to put people into patterns that work toward the benefit of the whole program.

- Never ask an employee to do a task that you wouldn't do yourself.
- Let staff see you clean the bathroom after a toilet overflows.
- Visit each classroom when you arrive in the morning and greet each staff member by name. Say hello to children.
- Highlight staff members' personal and professional accomplishments Use memos, family newsletters, or bulletin boards to display and acknowledge their accomplishments. For example, recognize Madison's unique bulletin board, Austin's completion of a first aid course, and Gabrielle's new grandmother status.
- Recognize longevity and loyalty with a progression of awards. For example, people who complete one year of employment might get a day off. After two years, they may get a designated parking space. For extensive longevity, consider naming a room after the employee. The yellow room can just as easily be called Ms. Rose's Room or the kitchen Alice's Place.

Relating to others is defined as a director's ability to really know staff, families, and children. It requires a commitment to mutual support as well as an awareness of the possibility that not all staff will be successful.

- Temporarily move struggling employees to a room with a seasoned staff member. A picture is worth a thousand words. Walking in the shoes of a successful person can help the employee get a feel for what works.

- Involve staff in decision making. It is a true statement about human behavior that what we help build, we are far more likely to support. If there is money available for equipment or supplies, ask for staff input on how to spend it.
- Involve staff in setting policy. Classroom teachers, for example, may recognize that a particular policy regarding show-and-tell is disruptive to the class schedule and should be changed.
- Plan an orientation period for all new employees. Offer opportunities to visit other classrooms. Meet with new employees on a regular basis to check on their progress.

Subjects & Predicates

Understanding children means being aware of behavior and the steps of child development, which results in the ability to plan curriculum appropriate to children's needs. Directors utilize this knowledge to help educate families and staff to work effectively with children.

- Stay abreast of current research and literature pertaining to early childhood and child care practices.
- Attend local, regional, and national conferences and workshops.
- Develop a network of friends in the field of early childhood. It is important to have someone you can bounce ideas off.
- Join early childhood professional organizations.
- Offer family workshops and seminars.
- Develop a newsletter for families to keep them informed and help educate them about current parenting practices.

Understanding self refers to a director's concept of his or her own values, attitudes, strengths, weaknesses, and goals. To direct others, a person must have a strong sense of self.

- Model the behavior that you expect from others.
- Develop core values (a code by which to live and work) that represent your aspirations for your center, the staff who work there, the children who come there to learn and play, and the families who trust you with their most precious possessions—their children. Core values provide clear objectives for all employees. They also send a strong message to the families and the community about your center goals.
- Be reflective. Take time to review your actions of the day. Think about ways to improve. Pat yourself on the back for things that go well.

Recommended Reading

Blanchard, K. & S. Johnson. (1993). *The one minute manager*. New York: Berkley.

Brazelton, T.B & S.I. Greenspan. (2000). *The irreducible needs of children: What every child must have to grow, learn, and flourish*. Cambridge, MA: Perseus Books.

Brazelton, T.B. (1994). *Touchpoints: Your child's emotional and behavioral development*. Cambridge, MA: Perseus Books.

Collins, J.C. & J.I. Porras. (1997). *Built to last: Successful habits of visionary companies*. New York: Harper Business.

Covey, S.R. (1989). *The 7 habits of highly effective people*. New York: Simon & Schuster, Inc.

Goleman, D. (1997). *Emotional intelligence*. New York: Bantam Books.

Gordon, T. (1986). *Leader effectiveness training, L.E.T: The no-lose way to the productive potential of people*. New York: Bantam.

Healy, J.M. (1987). *Your child's growing mind: A guide to learning and brain development from birth to adolescence*. New York: Doubleday.

Kotter, J.P. (1999). *What leaders really do*. Boston, MA: Harvard Business School Press.

Peters, T. & N. Austin. (1989). *A passion for excellence: The leadership difference*. New York: Warner Books.

Peters, T. (1994). *The pursuit of WOW!* New York: Vintage Books.

Schiller, P. (1999). *Start smart: Building brain power in the early years*. Beltsville, MD: Gryphon House.

Schiller, P. & T. Bryant. (1998). *The values book*. Beltsville, MD: Gryphon House.

Internet Resources

Children, Youth and Families Education and Research Network (CyferNet).
URL http://www.cyfernet.org
Links to professional organizations, electronic mail groups, program management resources.

ERIC Educational Resources Information Center and ERIC/EECE Clearinghouse on Elementary and Early Childhood Education.
URL http://www.ericeece.org
A national information system supported by the U.S. Department of Education. Database with search, publications on child care quality, LISTSERV discussion groups, resource lists, conference calendar.

National Association for the Education of Young Children (NAEYC).
URL http://naeyc.org
Professional development, accreditation, conferences, publications, membership, journal *Young Children* with searchable index, scholarly journal *Early Childhood Research Quarterly* with "Practitioners Perspectives." Online catalog of books, videotapes, brochures, and other resources.

National Child Care Information Center (NCCIC).
URL http://www.nccic.org
Large body of resources on quality child care.

National Network for Child Care (NNCC)
URL http://www.nncc.org
This site aims to "make quality research, resources, and best practices available nationally for local access." Articles, assistance from child care experts, state licensing information and statistics, discussion forum, conference listings. Sponsored by the Cooperative State Research, Education, and Extension Service and the U.S. Department of Agriculture.

U.S. Small Business Administration (SBA) (1999). *How to Start a Quality Child Care Business*. Management and Planning Series Publication MP-29.
URL http://www.sba.gov/library/pubs/mp-29.doc

Child Care Director's Job Description

- Ensure compliance with local, state, and federal regulations.

- Prepare manuals and policy and procedure statements.

- Ensure the development of record keeping systems essential to effective administrative and program operation.

- Develop inventory control practices for property, nonexpendable equipment, and expendable supplies.

- Develop and periodically review an effective, efficient administrative structure and staffing plan that delineates and defines departmental and position functions.

- Develop and periodically review a wage and salary program that ensures similar remuneration for comparable responsibility, education, and experience.

- Ensure the preparation of written personnel policies and practices and center-wide adherence to them.

- Supervise all personnel, paid and volunteer, assigned to the center.

- Hire, orient, evaluate the performance of, make salary adjustments for, and terminate personnel.

- Develop in-service training.

- Develop and execute an ongoing program that contributes to the growth and development of children.

- Maintain a physical environment that conforms to governmental standards of safety and cleanliness.

- Enroll children and establish fees to be paid by families according to center policy.

- Collect and record fees.

- Develop and administer the budget.

- Schedule assignments of personnel.

- Plan and conduct regular staff meetings.

Inventory of Director's Managerial Skills

Rate yourself on each statement, using the following scale:

❶ Strongly Disagree   ❷ Disagree   ❸ Neutral   ❹ Agree   ❺ Strongly Agree

_____ 1. I look for potential in my staff.

_____ 2. I really care about my staff as people with dignity and value.

_____ 3. I know the strengths of each staff member and plan for staff to work in areas where they feel successful.

_____ 4. My staff knows I want to help them.

_____ 5. I know the children in the center and am sensitive to their individual needs.

_____ 6. I really work to know and understand my staff.

_____ 7. My staff knows I want this center to be an active and creative environment.

_____ 8. I have a clear understanding of my basic responsibilities as a child care director.

_____ 9. I am computer literate.

_____ 10. I stay abreast of child development news information.

_____ 11. I spend time listening to my staff.

_____ 12. I know my strengths and weaknesses and work toward new strengths.

_____ 13. I help families understand curriculum.

_____ 14. I encourage staff to act on their ideas, and give support when possible.

_____ 15. I enjoy my work.

_____ 16. I am enthusiastic and my staff knows I am enthusiastic.

_____ 17. I help families understand the behavior of their children.

_____ 18. I am consistent and remain true to my convictions.

_____ 19. I involve staff in decision making.

_____ 20. I have a clearly conceptualized set of values.

_____ 21. I enjoy and cultivate a sense of humor.

_____ 22. I let my staff know they are really needed.

_____ 23. I am willing to spend the time necessary to be an outstanding child care director.

_____ 24. I try to generate new ideas that are beneficial to the center, children, and staff.

_____ 25. I believe that staff can have potential for growth and that appropriate in-service education can encourage this process.

Scoring Key

Commitment: statements 1, 6, 8, 9, 11, 18, 23, 24

Delegation: statements 2, 3, 4, 14, 19, 22, 25

Motivation: statements 7, 16, 21, 24

Understanding children: statements 5, 10, 13, 17

Understanding self: statements 12, 15, 17, 20

0-2: Area of Concern

3: Possible Concern

4-5: Area of strength

Management Techniques

2

Management techniques are critical to the success of a child care center. Even the best plans, if poorly implemented, can lead to frustration and, ultimately, failure of the center. Think through your philosophies and make practical use of the worksheets provided in this chapter. This, coupled with your unique abilities, will lead to a more effective organization.

Nancy Alexander

Decision Making

Decision making can be defined as making a conscious choice after careful consideration of several alternatives. A decision by the manager commits the center to a given course of action. The outcomes of the decision-making process affect center policies, personnel rules, development of long-range goals, commitment of resources, and direction of curriculum. The importance of skill in this area cannot be minimized; the topic deserves your special consideration.

Decision making is *action oriented*. An action may result from several minor decisions or one major decision. The process of making choices seems simple, but what makes it complex is weighing information (checking resources and consequences) related to each possible alternative, and then selecting one alternative that will produce the anticipated results. The prediction of likely consequences associated with each possibility, the checking of resources, and the recognition of accountability regardless of outcome make the decision-making process an awesome responsibility.

Many experts believe that problem solving, decision making, and creativity are essentially the same process. Each is viewed as a form of thinking, with the primary difference being the result. Creativity is thinking that produces ideas, decision making results in a choice among alternative courses of action, and problem solving is finding a solution to a dilemma. In the field of child care, there is a tendency to perceive all three areas as decision making.

Steps in Decision Making

Over the years, educators, philosophers, social scientists, and writers have each tried to describe the steps in the decision-making process. Basically the steps they have defined are similar, except for the use of different words or a slight expansion of the steps (see Problem Solving Chart on page 44).

Decision-Making Process in Child Care

1. Identify and clarify the problem in your own mind.
2. Call together all the people involved in the problem (and only those people).
3. Define the problem and get general agreement from all those involved that there is a problem. (You may have to backtrack here and restate some goals with which the problem is in conflict.)
4. Generate solutions—solicit from others all possible ideas, and contribute solutions yourself only if the others seem to be missing something obvious. Write down the suggestions.
5. Decide which is the best solution.
6. Check resources.
7. Write down a plan for implementation (i.e., who specifically will do what and when).
8. Determine what support will be needed from you, such as supplies, time, and so on.
9. Decide when and how to evaluate the solution.
10. Reconvene. If the problem has been solved, celebrate. If not, evaluate what went wrong with the first plan. Then, begin the process again. Even if a workable solution is hard to find, knowing that you are earnestly seeking one will help reduce frustration. It's the feeling that nobody knows or cares about a problem that causes people to give up in despair.

The first three steps of the process probably require sensitivity more than any other skill. You must clearly see the need for a decision, including all related components. For example, let's look at the need for family involvement in the child care center. You must first recognize that the need exists and that it will require a change in behavior and attitude of both staff and families. Therefore, you will probably want to get input from both staff members and families.

The search for solutions (step 4) is the creative element in the decision-making process. In this example, there are several ways in which families can become involved in the program, such as an advisory council, volunteer programs, and family education seminars. Solicit as many solutions or alternatives as possible from staff and families and add any obvious possibilities that are missing. You can facilitate this step by changing attitudes and habits that create barriers and by searching for fresh viewpoints. You should even examine what seem to be "wild" ideas, such as family members filling in for staff on a staff member's birthday.

The fifth step, deciding which is the best solution, is the most difficult. This is when you must project the probable consequences of each alternative in a way that helps you compare the possible courses of action and select the best alternatives. You have used other participants in the preceding steps, but now the final decision is yours. You will ultimately be held accountable for your choice. Selection is basically a reduction process. First, you must consider the cost-effectiveness of each alternative, remembering that cost includes dollars, time, human resources, and possible trade-offs. Personal value judgments will surely come into play during this part of the decision-making process—they may be either helpful or harmful. In some cases, past experience might prove helpful in reaching a decision. Other times, previous negative experiences will make you leery of choosing a potentially productive solution. Your personal values are important—just be sure you recognize them.

Checking resources (the sixth step) is also important. A reasonable solution to unsafe playground equipment might be to purchase new equipment. However, if your budget won't allow it, this solution is not a valid one.

As you prepare a plan for implementation (the seventh step), you must be very specific. This step will automatically move you into the eighth step, examining your resources and determining what support you will have to give to the project. A form such as the one on page 45 (Implementation Plan) will assist you in preparing an implementation plan. If a goal requires more than one strategy to be implemented, place them in order of priority.

The ninth step is determining a method of evaluation. All skilled decision makers evaluate their decisions. You will want others to help in the evaluation process. Sometimes you will feel that your course of action was incorrect and consequently find yourself back at the first step. Or you may find that your solution is only a band-aid or temporary fix, and you will need to go through the process again in order to search for a more permanent solution. Decision making is a continuous process, not just the final act. Each step is important to the outcome. Evaluating outcomes is usually the most neglected part of the decision-making process. However, you can learn from your mistakes and save time in the future if you follow through by determining the value of your decisions.

Nancy Alexander

Solving Problems

Let us consider some problems that are common in most child care centers. We'll use the outlined process (page 21) as a guide to resolving these difficulties.

Problem: *Late Arrival of Classroom Teacher*

1. According to the staff sign-in sheet and observations by administration, families, and staff, a classroom teacher has been arriving late about 40 percent of the time.
2. Schedule an appointment with the teacher to discuss this problem. If you verbally set up the meeting, also follow up with a written memo noting the time and place of the meeting. The tone of the memo should convey that the purpose of the meeting is to find a solution to the late arrivals, not for disciplinary action.
3. At the meeting, be specific about the number of times the teacher has been late, and together, explore the consequences (for example,

unsupervised children, unhappy families, a negative start to the day for both families and the teacher, and most important, the breach of the original contract regarding arrival time).

4. Ask the teacher for some ideas about how to get to the center on time and write them down. If necessary, add some of your own ideas.

5. Reach an agreed-upon arrival time.

6. Put the plan in written form.

7. Be specific about any involvement you will have in the success of the plan, such as dealing with families who arrive before the designated opening of the classroom.

8. Set a date for evaluating the success of the plan. If the teacher is successful, be sure to show approval; if not, do not hesitate to start the process again.

Problem: *Family-Child Separation Problem*

1. A classroom teacher has come to you with a problem concerning separation anxiety. The teacher has observed the child's mother standing in the hall looking upset. The child has difficulty entering the classroom and usually cries for approximately 20 minutes after the mother leaves.

2. Arrange a meeting with the family and the teacher. Ask the teacher to be prepared by writing down any of his or her observations.

3. Ask for input from the family regarding the situation. (How does the day at home begin? Discuss the reactions of the mother and child when they arrive at the center. What factors may be contributing to the problem at home and/or at the center?) For example, the mother may explain that she has been feeling guilty about her return to work, and that her mother-in-law told her, "I don't see how you can leave that beautiful child with strangers." She may also say that the teacher has sometimes been unavailable to greet and take the child at the door.

4. Try to get both the mother and father involved in finding a solution to the problem. For example, they may try to:
   - Get to know the center staff better.
   - Encourage the child to bring a familiar item from home to the center for nap time, such as a favorite storybook or stuffed animal.
   - Encourage the child to make friends among the other children, and perhaps even play with them away from the center.

5. Decide which is the best course of action.

6. Write down the plan. An example might be:
   - The mother will take two hours away from her job to come and visit the center—perhaps to do a simple cooking project with the children if cooking is her hobby. This way she will learn more about the center's daily routine, become familiar with the staff, and feel more comfortable knowing that her child is in a warm, caring environment in her absence.
   - The teacher will keep open the lines of communication by sending occasional notes home about what has happened during the day.
   - The parents will alternate mornings bringing the child to the center.
   - The teacher will make every effort to be readily available to greet the child upon arrival to the classroom, and the parents will leave at an agreed-upon time.
   - The teacher will introduce the parents to the parents of their child's classroom friend, with the possibility of a visit outside the center.

7. Determine what necessary support might be needed from you as director. In this case, you need to assure the teacher that an aide will be available at the designated arrival time so that she or he will be free to greet the child at the door.

8. Set a date to evaluate the progress of the plan and, if necessary, to rework a plan of action. Your sensitive responses to the parents' feelings, the teacher's dilemma, and the growth of the child's sense of security will provide an atmosphere for a successful solution to this problem.

Problem: *Poor Classroom Management Techniques, Leading to Center Disruption*

1. Special teachers (music and physical education) at the center have reported that Classroom B's teacher is not getting the children to their classes on time, neighboring classroom teachers complain that the noise level from Classroom B interferes with their class activities, an aide from Classroom B has requested reassignment to a new group, and your observation of this classroom leads you to believe that there is a problem with the teacher's management techniques.

2. Arrange a meeting with the teacher of Classroom B, the aide, the special teachers, and the teachers from the two adjacent classrooms. There are

already six people involved in this particular problem. If you do not take action soon, you may have families involved as well—a compelling reason not to procrastinate!

3. Start by stating the specific problems that were brought to your attention. Then, making sure to involve all present, discuss the implications of these problems on the smooth running of the center as a whole, the effect on schedules, and so on.

4. During the discussion, someone may suggest that the teacher begin preparing to leave the classroom about ten minutes before the end of class so that the children arrive at the gym or music room on time.

5. Discuss the causes for the extra noise in the classroom and ways to avoid some of it (for example, the teacher can try not to call across the room to a child, try to lower her or his own voice, and monitor how many children are using each activity center).

6. Offer the teacher a program of selected reading materials on classroom management, seminars at local community colleges, observance of other classrooms, and other specific suggestions. Encouraging feedback between the teacher and yourself is critical.

7. Suggest that the teacher include the aide in planning daily activities and discuss the aide's involvement in these activities.

8. Write down ideas, making sure that there is a clear understanding of them. For example, ideas may include implementing a new schedule the week after the meeting, with all staff being informed two days in advance; meeting with the teacher one hour a week to help with and discuss classroom management techniques; and having two teachers provide an in-service program for all staff on classroom management.

9. When the plan has been agreed upon by all, you will be assured that the teacher will be meeting with the aide at least once a week to discuss programs and delegation of duties, you will be meeting with the teacher once a week to work on classroom management ideas and skills, and a new schedule will be distributed by an agreed-upon date.

10. All those involved in this meeting will meet again in one month to evaluate the plan's progress.

Time Management

When the subject of time management is mentioned in a group of child care center directors, the response is usually skeptical smiles. The doubt is understandable when you consider a director's typical day. Interruptions are too numerous to count. However, if there is a place where time management will pay off, it is in the child care center.

Public relations are a large part of the fiscal success of a center. Directors need to handle a variety of demands on their time, while at the same time present an image of competence and efficiency. They are, after all, selling a program.

It is not unusual to arrive at work to find that a planned schedule, such as mailing financial statements, interviewing to fill a new staff position, and setting up a field trip for the preschool, must also include finding a substitute for the next day, answering a phone call from an unhappy parent, purchasing supplies for a special art project, arranging for the repair of a refrigerator that is not cooling, and meeting with a parent who drops in without an appointment to talk with you about the center program.

Time management is a serious subject. It means getting things done. Keep in mind that people who produce are more apt to reach their goals both professionally and personally.

There is a difference between being busy and being effective. All child care directors are busy people. For example, consider Richele, a director who comes into her office, answers the phone, and takes a message for a teacher. She hand delivers the message to the classroom and on the way back, stops to get a cup of coffee, which she takes to the office. She starts to go through the mail and sees something of interest for the music teacher. She takes it to her and stays to chat for a few minutes. If you were to drop into this center, you would think Richele is a busy person, but in reality, she is not accomplishing much.

Take a look at yourself. When is the last time you set personal and professional goals for yourself? If you invest the time in planning, for each minute you spend now, you'll save lots of minutes later. Think about the goals that you would like to achieve in the next year. To help you focus on your goals, list them under the four categories of Personal Growth, Career, Material, and Other (see example on page 46).

Keep in mind that time management will be useful in every area of your life and should result in more available time. What will you do with this time? Hopefully the answer is that you will steadily make progress toward getting what you want out of life.

You need to evaluate the way you establish priorities and the way you approach tasks. For instance, do you think that if you do all the little jobs first, you will then have time for the high priority ones? If you do, stop now. It doesn't work this way!

Set your goal, determine which project will help you reach that goal, break the project down into several steps, and establish a priority rating. The last time you started a new project, did you select the job that needed to be done first or the one that was most interesting to do?

Let's take a look at how you rate in time management. Complete the Inventory of Time Management Behavior and Techniques on page 47, and use the information to plan a strategy for change, if needed.

Organizational Help

Let's begin with how to make a list. Take a piece of paper and make three headings (leave sufficient space after each one): Things To Do, Places To Go, and Phone Calls To Make.

First, list the things you have been planning to do but have been putting off for a long time. Now set it aside, and prepare a record of what happened yesterday. Start with the time you woke up and record what you did all day, in half-hour segments (for example, 6:00 a.m., 6:30 a.m., 7:00 a.m., and so on), until you went to bed. Try to remember all the little things that happened during the day. This activity is a difficult task, but it will sharpen your ability to pay attention to all the time you have available and to look realistically at how you are using this precious time.

Now you need to plan a day, remembering to break down each job into components. Figure out a deadline for completion of each component. Make sure to allow some additional time so you won't be frustrated if you are interrupted. Try to plan your day following the example of a Daily Plan on page 48.

Once you have planned your day, check back and see whether you have incorporated the items from your "Things To Do" list. If you have avoided listing them, what are the reasons? Are you a procrastinator? Take a closer look by completing the "quiz" on page 49 (Inventory of Attitudes Toward Completion of Tasks).

When you have completed this self-evaluation, look for ways to improve your completion of tasks. For example, if you do your best work in the morning, use this time to tackle the job you dislike doing most. Prepare a schedule that best suits your needs and the way you work most effectively. Adhere to this schedule as closely as possible.

Record Keeping

Organization of office space goes hand in hand with better use of time. Here is a method to clear your desk of clutter. Sort your papers into four piles. In the first pile, put the papers that require your action—these are the current projects. The second pile should consist of papers that you'll be sending to other people. In the third pile, put all the items that need to be filed. Finally, place all reading materials in the fourth pile, and remove them from your desk.

Reorganize the pile of current projects according to priority and keep these in a folder on your desk. Designate another space, such as a desk drawer, for the work that will need your attention next. This is your future file.

Use your desk calendar to record such notes as due dates for reports, various reminders, and needed information about your

Subjects & Predicates

appointments. This cuts down on the stack of memos and little slips of paper cluttering your desk. You can also use the calendar to note the date to begin work on a report so it will be ready on schedule. (Of course, the due date will also be on your calendar.)

Clearing up your desk area is one of the hardest tasks to master, but it can be done. Whatever method you use, don't neglect the routine or you'll soon find yourself back in the same boat. Messiness is sometimes equated with getting a lot of work done, but this is not necessarily the case. In fact, from a public relations point of view, an attractive office sets a positive tone for prospective users of your service. Use your wastebasket. If you have any doubt at all about the need for a piece of paper, this is the signal to throw it away.

Keep in mind that record keeping is an ongoing part of your duties. The three elements involved are: constantly collecting information, putting it somewhere, and trying to find it again.

Why is it necessary to address this segment of business administration? One important reason is to comply with state licensing regulations, which require that you keep certain documents on hand. Another reason is to meet the legal ramifications of personnel issues and family concerns. Last, and most obvious, record keeping is necessary to run your center smoothly and effectively, which results in better use of time, higher income for your center, and more energy and time available for pursuits away from work.

Records management begins at the time you obtain information. You must make an on-the-spot judgment as to its value, and it must have a purpose if you are to keep it.

One method to ensure the collection of pertinent data is to develop standard forms, which should be multipurpose whenever possible. (See page 50 for an example of an index card to keep by the office telephone.) The use of forms keeps words to a minimum. Keep in mind that storage of records costs money. New technologies have evolved to help with the increasing volume of paperwork. Study the costs of a copier and consider the value of a computer and storage on discs.

Look over your files and separate anything not likely to be used in the next six months. These records can go into dead storage. You may need to find something in a hurry some day! Again, if you cannot define a real purpose for something, throw it out. Always keep official documents, such as directives from funding or regulatory agencies, and minutes of meetings of governing boards.

Below is a list of categories that you can use to organize your records. Of course, you may not need all the suggested headings in your center. Select those that are pertinent to your programs. The list shows the documents that you would file under each category.

Board Records
- Minutes of all meetings
- Correspondence copies of resolutions and recommendations
- Names, addresses, and phone numbers of members
- Terms of office and positions held
- Charter and articles of incorporation
- List of members of appointed committees

Family Day Home Records
(These records are needed when a center uses family day homes as an adjunct to its programs.)
- Evaluation of family day homes
- Fee arrangements
- Licenses issued
- Conferences with day home mothers and with families who use the family day home
- Attendance records
- Accident reports
- Lists of equipment lent to day home mothers and summaries of training sessions
- Lists of children in day homes, including start and termination dates
- Correspondence

Business Management Records
Accounting and Budget
- Duplicate receipts of fee payments, any adjustments or waivers of fees

- Reports of fees due and fees paid
- Reports of fees owed, reason for nonpayment, and plan for collection of outstanding fees

Income and Expense Statements
- Budget analysis of income and expenditures
- Program budgets
- Balance sheet showing assets and liabilities
- Line item budget, with total income, expenses, and cost per child
- Records on all line items of the operating budget
- Copies of cost control practices and procedures
- Minutes of meetings dealing with budget development, review, and approval
- Correspondence relating to the above

Payroll
- Salaries, including regular and substitute staff
- Fringe benefits (workman's compensation, health and accident insurance, retirement program, unemployment insurance)
- Reimbursable expenses (in-service training, travel expenses, and conference attendance)
- Internal Revenue Service (W-4 forms for each employee, IRS W-2 forms for each employee, IRS reporting forms, copies of current IRS and Social Security tax regulations)
- Time sheets for each employee
- Written authorization for deductions other than those required by law
- Authorization for the hiring of each employee
- Authorization for any pay change for each employee
- Dates of vacation and sick time
- Record of any overtime worked
- Mailing addresses of any employees terminated during the year

Health Records (confidential)
- Health records of employees, including TB test results
- Record of health policies
- Each child's medical history (medical examinations, immunization records, hearing and visual testing results, dental examinations,

records of any health or physical problems such as allergies, reports of treatment by physicians, accident reports, reports of conferences with families on health-related issues)
- Records of extermination of vermin and rodents
- Directives from the regulatory agency, such as sanitizing procedures for food service equipment
- Nutritional information, such as menus of meals and snacks
- Food service procedures
- Written records of approval of a physician for special therapeutic diets

Safety Records
- Records of safety practices (emergency evacuation and relocation plans for fire, explosion, toxic fumes, or other chemical release; plans for periodic renovation of facilities and indoor and outdoor equipment; plans for storage of dangerous materials)
- Records of accidents
- Records of maintenance work, renovation, and equipment replacement
- Records of inspections, recommendations, and directives by regulatory agency personnel
- Record of first aid equipment
- Records of any licenses or reports issued by regulatory agencies, such as the fire marshal, sanitation inspectors, and gas pipe inspectors

Employee Benefit Records
- Copies of current medical, retirement, and life insurance program information, including fees
- Correspondence relating to payroll
- Applications for employment

Personnel (personal and confidential)
- Record of interview for hire
- References
- Reports relating to health
- Record of dates of hire and termination

- Performance evaluations
- Record of any change in educational status, salary adjustments, transfers, promotions, and so on
- Record of any in-service training provided to employee
- Reports of conferences with the employee
- Information the employee wishes to have included in his or her personnel file
- Record of exit interview
- Any correspondence relating to the employee
- Personnel policies
- Job description for each position in center
- Plan of orientation for new employees

Program Records

- Program content and activities for children
- Objectives of program for each area of development: physical, social, emotional, and intellectual
- Statement of objectives of the program for home-school relationships
- Children's progress reports and group progress reports
- Family's comments about program
- Records of effectiveness of program
- Correspondence pertaining to safety issues

Social Services Records (family history; confidential)

- Record of referral procedures
- Listings of community service agencies
- Release forms required for transmittal of pertinent confidential information
- Signed release forms and copies of information sent to anyone outside the center
- Records of referrals to community services
- Summaries of home visits
- Summaries of case conferences held on behalf of families
- Summaries of conferences and counseling sessions held with family members

Psychological Service Records (confidential)
- Reports of diagnostic tests
- Release of information forms
- Signed release forms and copies of information sent
- Summaries of treatment sessions
- Summaries of consultations and conferences
- Reports of observations and recommendations about program adjustments
- Summaries of staff training sessions conducted by psychologists
- All correspondence related to the above

Volunteer Records
- Description of volunteer program
- Copy of reference manual for volunteers
- Applications of volunteers
- Summaries of orientation and training sessions
- Summaries of conferences with volunteers
- Assignments: person filling position, date of assignment, transfers, and terminations
- Evaluations of volunteers' performance (confidential)
- List of groups or organizations that provide volunteers
- Paperwork required by participating organizations
- Correspondence relating to the volunteer program

Interruptions

Interruptions are difficult for any manager, but they are particularly difficult in the world of child care, where the unexpected is expected. Imagine how much work you could accomplish if you had large blocks of uninterrupted time. Fortunately, there are effective techniques you can use that will result in the time you need for planning and goal setting for your center. In other words, the objective is to have time to do the work of the director, rather than of the staff. This indicates a need to train staff to take responsibility for their own work, and to meet with the staff in the initial stages to be sure the project goals are clear and then again later to evaluate the progress.

One kind of interruption is self-interruption. Every time you take an extended lunch or coffee break, or do work that should be done by another, you are interfering with your own job. Of course, interruption must be accepted as part of the job. For example, crises such as injury to a child or staff member certainly need your immediate response. In addition, families under stress, perhaps because of a concern about their child's situation in the center, should know that you will give them your attention. Also, staff members who have unusual problems need to know you are available. However, you should examine your open-door policy and be sure you are not using it as a way for both you and your staff to avoid work!

If you are serious about reducing interruptions, learn to assert yourself. If you have trouble saying no, examine your reluctance—time management means saying no to others as well as to yourself. Assertiveness is tactful, mature, patient behavior. It is an attitude that enhances debate, using logic and facts with a cooperative spirit. Be careful, however, not to use remarks that put people on the defensive, which often spoils the chance of successful negotiation. Learn to say no for a reason and say it with tact and courtesy. Remember to use signals, such as rising from your chair when you feel the need to end the conference. Walk the person to the door and suggest that he or she makes an appointment for another meeting, if you feel it is necessary. Your attitude will be admired, and hopefully your staff will model your behavior.

Delegation

An important part of management is to know when and how to delegate work to others. The role of the manager is to get things done—to accomplish certain goals through delegating work to others.

Effective Delegation of Work

1. Evaluate your staff in order to know their strengths, growth potential areas, and learning styles. Ask each staff member to complete the Staff Evaluation Worksheet on page 51.

2. Provide the necessary training based on your observations of staff needs and staff's evaluation of their own needs.

3. Make a list of all the areas in which you work and decide which tasks you can assign to others.

4. Be sure you give authority to the person who will be carrying out the assignment.

5. Explain clearly the work that must be done, along with a deadline for each segment of the project. Ask for the work to be completed before your deadline so that there will be time for any adjustments that may be needed.

6. Encourage your staff to evaluate their own work and give them opportunities to learn from their mistakes. Hold people accountable for results.

7. Be sure your expectations are reasonable. Since you are not doing the job, it may not be done exactly as you would have done it.

8. Remember that recognition given in front of peers, responsibility, challenge, and autonomy are all rewards that help staff grow and remain content in their work.

Following the above steps will strengthen your entire organization. It will also ensure that you have time to do your own work.

Telephone Techniques

Staff with good telephone skills are an asset to your program. The telephone is only as helpful as the person who controls it. Using the telephone effectively will add another positive dimension to your management of time. Keep in mind that many calls can be handled by staff other than yourself.

The staff member delegated to answer the telephone in your center should be fully aware of the public relations aspect of this responsibility and should be knowledgeable about which areas of information are handled by particular staff members. The person answering the phone can then direct the call

Subjects & Predicates

appropriately or, when advisable, answer the caller's questions directly, without interrupting you. If you are expecting an urgent or V.I.P. call, let the person who answers the phone know. If the initial contact is solid, it will save you time in later interviews, because the caller will already feel comfortable with your professionalism. Often the first contact with your organization will take place by telephone. Listed below are some simple rules for your staff to follow:

Effective Telephone Techniques

1. Begin by identifying the center by name in a pleasant tone.
2. Be sure to write down the name and phone number of the caller and the purpose of the call.
3. Note the best time for a return call; this will cut down on frustration for both the caller and the person who will return the call.

When you call others, group your calls and make as many as you can in one sitting as early in the day as possible. Have your materials for each call close at hand, with an outline of what you want to cover. How many times have you hung up the phone only to remember something you didn't say? Having an outline keeps this from happening. Also, writing notes on your outline as you talk will provide a record of the call for your files.

Control the length of the call by your tone of voice. Be businesslike. Cultivate a pleasant tone and speak clearly and distinctly. When you leave a message, always ask that your call be returned by a definite date and time.

Meetings

Positive responses to meetings can be set in motion by careful, knowledgeable planning that begins with establishing the need for the meeting. The reason for a meeting should in some way relate to implementing the goals of your center. If it doesn't, then a meeting may not be necessary.

Once the reason for the meeting has been established, you need to consider who should attend. Be sure that each person invited has some relevance to the subject being covered. Send out an agenda early enough so persons attending will be prepared to participate in the meeting. Choose a meeting site that also suits the agenda. For instance, if attendees will be doing a lot of writing or note taking, you will want to select a place with a conference table. In addition, the surroundings should be conducive to participation. Be sure to start the meeting on time. This will let others know they need to be on time.

You should always assign someone to take minutes, regardless of the size of the group or type of meeting. These minutes need to be transcribed and sent to all participants after the meeting.

Nancy Alexander

The chairperson is one of the keys to a successful meeting. As chairperson, you need to be skilled at soliciting participation and, at the same time, setting limits in order to focus on the purpose of the meeting. Begin by explaining the areas you wish to cover. Encourage involvement in a nonjudgmental way. Are you expecting formal presentations by different members, brainstorming (the free association of ideas, with people giving their responses at random), or discussion? Most meetings are a combination of these approaches. The task of the chairperson is to continually focus on the goals, while encouraging questions and the contribution of ideas, solutions, and criticisms.

Remember that whenever you bring people together, there is a real possibility that personality differences will cause conflicts. Most group leaders need to learn how to handle the monopolizer. Once it is clear that you have a group member who talks too much, you must handle the problem. If not, you will lose the rest of the group. Of course, you should avoid embarrassing the monopolizer in front of the others. An effective technique is to avoid making eye contact so that he or she will be recognized less often. Break in when the person is speaking, with a comment such as, "That's an interesting idea; let's hear what everyone else thinks about it." If you continue to have difficulty with this person, meet with him or her in private and explain that you are trying to draw out ideas from everyone and ask for the monopolizer's help. This usually works.

If you have the opposite problem—too many silent or withdrawn members— ask yourself if they really have an interest in or can contribute to the session. If the answer is yes, be sure that the atmosphere is nonthreatening. When quiet persons feel safe, they are more likely to participate. This problem relates to the people who should be invited to your meetings. With the right mixture of people and strong leadership, you will have lively, productive sessions.

Meeting Checklist

1. Establish the need for a meeting.
2. Invite the appropriate people.
3. Send each member a reminder of the time and place and an agenda.
4. Choose a place that will facilitate the type of meeting being held.
5. Start and end on time.
6. Take minutes.
7. Stick to business.
8. Schedule another meeting, if necessary.
9. Send minutes to all participants after the meeting.

Stress in the Child Care Profession

Because stress directly relates to our effectiveness in all areas of our lives, we need to consider our personal responses to the enormous pressures of modern society. As center directors, you are expected to meet the needs of the children enrolled, their families, and the center staff. This in itself is a demanding job. Add to it the pressures of your own family situation and personal life, and you will realize that for the sake of your health you cannot ignore this subject.

As you consider the impact of your fast-paced life on your physical and emotional health, you can readjust your methods of coping, where needed. Use the Stress Buster Checklist on page 52 as a guide.

A good place to start is to evaluate your workspace. You need a pleasant atmosphere in which to work. You can make even the smallest place look more inviting. For example, if you like flowers, occasionally invest in a flowering plant. You'll cheer up not only yourself but your staff as well. In any case, place something you really enjoy looking at in your office. Get rid of clutter. Clutter is depressing and makes your work seem overwhelming. A pleasant working environment improves a person's disposition.

Set aside some time for yourself. If you have a hobby such as needlepoint, work on it during your lunch hour. Or take a walk at lunchtime. Any exercise you do during the day will help counteract the effects of stress. You'll feel better when you return to work and consequently will do a better job. Try getting up a little earlier in the morning to work out, take a bike ride, or go for a fast walk.

If you find getting up early is difficult, try going to bed earlier. A great way to relax is to take a long, warm bubble bath. Make arrangements for someone else to be "on call" for your family, if this is a problem, and soak away your tension.

Even at your desk, there are some techniques you can use to relieve tension. Stretching, rolling your shoulders, and yawning take only a minute or two. When your eyes ache, use palming: Cover your eyes with your palms so no light comes through and rest the heels of your hands lightly on your cheekbones. Let your mind go to a place where you feel comfortable and relaxed. Spend at least two or three minutes in this state. Of course, there are many techniques for total body relaxation, and you can find various books on the subject.

Watch your diet—you can tell if you react to too much fat, sugar, or salt in your diet. Remember, "You are what you eat." Drink plenty of water, too. It keeps your brain alert.

As you become more in tune with yourself, you will begin to identify your stress levels. A small amount of stress keeps us on task, but too much stress is harmful to you. Find the right balance.

Review the section on assertiveness and consider how you can use this attitude to reduce stress. "Take one day at a time" is an old adage but this idea, coupled with the fact that "tomorrow is a new day," can give us a mind-set that will help us to shrug off all but the most serious difficulties. This is the same philosophy you want to relate to the children you serve.

Recommended Reading

Baldwin, S. (1996). *Lifesavers: Tips for success and sanity for early childhood managers*. St. Paul, MN: Redleaf Press.

Graft, R. (1990). *Preschool director's survival guide: 135 forms, checklists, letters, and guidelines for day-to-day management*. Upper Saddle River, NJ: Prentice Hall Trade.

Lowe, P. (1995). *Creativity and problem solving: Complete training package*. New York: McGraw-Hill Companies.

McGraw, P. (1999). *Life strategies: Doing what works, doing what matters*. New York: Hyperion.

Miller, E.E. (1997). *The 10-minute stress manager* {Audio Cassette}. Carlsbad, CA: Hay House, Inc.

Montanari, E.O. (1992). *101 ways to build enrollment in your early childhood program*. St. Paul, MN: Redleaf Press.

Rubin, M., P. Frahm, & P. Frahm. (1993). *60 ways to relieve stress in 60 seconds*. New York: Workman Publishing Company.

Schiller, P. *Start smart: Building brain power in the early years*. Beltsville, MD: Gryphon House.

Taylor, B. (1996). *Early childhood program management: People and procedures*. Upper Saddle River, NJ: Prentice Hall.

Internet Resources

Child Care Online.
http://www.childcare.net
Pruissen, C. (1999). *Caregiver Aids: Business Forms for Caregivers & Parents.*
Forms to calculate monthly income and expenses, attendance, and payment;
weekly activity and menu charts; personal child and family files; accident
reports; medication records; program planning schedules; and so on. Can be
ordered online.

*Daycare Forms Package: A Collection of the Most Commonly Used Forms in
Child Care* with software.
http://www.nationalchildcare.com/formspackage.htm

National Resource Center for Health and Safety in Child Care.
URL http://www.nrc.uchsc.edu
Child care links from A to Z. Links to individual states' child care licensure
regulations, national health and safety performance standards.

Software Providers – A number of software providers offer information on
child care center information management software (record keeping, child
and family information, health forms, reports, permission forms, contracts,
and so on). Some examples can be found at: URL
http://www.on-qsofttware.com,   http://www.childcareadmin.com,
http://www.providerware.com,   http://www.sba.gov/library/pubs/mp-30.doc,
http://www.daycaresoftware.com,   http://www.kasksoftware.com,
http://www.daycareorganizer.com

Problem Solving Chart

What's my
Problem?

What are my
Alternatives?

What strategy will
best meet my needs?

What resources do I have?

1. _____
2. _____
3. _____

What resources do I have?

1. _____
2. _____
3. _____

**What steps will complete
my strategy?**

1. _____
2. _____
3. _____

Implement Strategy

How can I check my
Decision?

Goal: To improve the sanitation of the center bathrooms

Implementation Plan

Strategies for Implementation	Resources Needed	Whose Responsibility	Time Frame
Observe the bathrooms periodically for three days	Time for custodian and staff to clean bathroom	Director	Day 1,2,3
Talk to custodian and develop a plan of action	Cleaning supplies	Director	Day 4
Meet with staff for input		Director and custodian	Day 5
One week of using new procedure		Custodian	Days 6-12
Follow-up meeting with custodian		Director	Day 13

Example of Goals in a One-Year Plan

Personal Growth

Develop charm

Be more loving

Become more self reliant

Career

Obtain promotion

Increase efficiency

Attend university classes in child development

Material

Plan regular maintenance on car

Paint living room

Buy a new winter coat

Other

Grow spiritually

Learn to knit

Take more time for leisure

Directions: Place a check mark under the appropriate selection.

	Often	Sometimes	Rarely
1. Do you write lists of work to be done?	☐	☐	☐
2. Do you establish a rating system, from high to low, for items on a priority list?	☐	☐	☐
3. Do you complete the items on your list by specific deadlines?	☐	☐	☐
4. Do you continue to review and update, in writing, your life goals (private and professional)?	☐	☐	☐
5. Is your work space attractive, uncluttered, and organized?	☐	☐	☐
6. Have you developed a filing system?	☐	☐	☐
7. Do you have techniques to deal with interruptions?	☐	☐	☐
8. Can you find items in your file quickly?	☐	☐	☐
9. Are you assertive?	☐	☐	☐
10. Do you plan uninterrupted work time during your day?	☐	☐	☐
11. Are you effective in keeping phone calls short?	☐	☐	☐
12. Do you work on preventing problems by using contingency planning?	☐	☐	☐
13. Do you use your time optimally?	☐	☐	☐
14. Can you pace yourself and plan your work to meet deadlines?	☐	☐	☐
15. Are you punctual?	☐	☐	☐
16. Do you get things done through others?	☐	☐	☐
17. Do subordinates cooperate with you when you delegate?	☐	☐	☐
18. Do you handle interruptions effectively?	☐	☐	☐
19. Do you work on the achievement of long-term goals?	☐	☐	☐
20. Are you aware of the most productive time of your day and do you plan your work to correlate?	☐	☐	☐
21. Do people know when to reach you?	☐	☐	☐
22. If you need to be absent from work, can someone else take over the project?	☐	☐	☐
23. Do you start and finish projects on time?	☐	☐	☐
24. Do you handle each piece of paper one time?	☐	☐	☐

Scoring Key

Here is how to mark your score:

Often   -   4 points
Sometimes -   2 points
Rarely   -   0 points

If your score was:

80-100   You manage your time very well and have control over most situations.

61-80   You manage well some of the time but need to be more consistent.

41-60   Techniques are needed to help you avoid what is going on around you and getting the best of you.

21-40   You are losing control and really need help.

0-20   You are overwhelmed, scattered, and frustrated. Are you under a lot of stress?

Daily Plan

URGENT: Interview candidate for infant room position

Order special materials for kindergarten teacher

Call Mrs. Jones to set up an appointment

HOURS:

7:30 A.M.	Arrive at center; unlock all rooms and cupboards
8:00	Greet staff/parents; check with assistant
8:30	Make phone calls (Mrs. Jones/supply company)
9:00	Note for teachers' boxes re: materials
9:30	Center walk-through
10:00	First interview scheduled
10:30	Candidate visit to infant room; write notes on interview
11:00	See first candidate off; second candidate interview
11:30	Visit classroom with second candidate
12:00 P.M.	See second candidate off; write notes on interview
12:30	Lunch with music supervisor
1:00	Open time
1:30	Third candidate interview
2:00	Third candidate visits classroom; write notes on interview
2:30	See third candidate off
3:00	Get feedback on candidates from infant room supervisor
3:30	Check with assistant director

Inventory of Attitudes Toward Completion of Tasks

Directions: Answer the following questions.

1. Why do I ignore certain tasks?
2. What are the consequences when I don't complete tasks?
3. What results when I do a job I would rather ignore?
4. At what time of day do I do my best work?
5. Do I have a clear idea of what needs to be done over a five-day work period?
6. Do I have an understanding of how long each job should take and do I set myself a "deadline?"
7. Do I view each new day as a "fresh start" and see my mistakes as opportunities to learn?

Index Card Containing Data on Child

Child's name _____ Group _____

Attendance schedule _____

Parents' names _____

Address _____

_____

Home/Work telephone #   H: _____

                               W: _____

Physician _____

Telephone #: _____

Allergies _____

_____

Person to call in emergency _____

Persons authorized to pick up child _____

_____   _____

Staff Evaluation Worksheet

1. How do you prefer to learn?

☐ Hands-on experience   ☐ Learning from previous encounters

2. What is most important to you?

☐ Being right   ☐ Meeting a deadline   ☐ Listening to others

3. How do you begin a task?

☐ Trial and error   ☐ Being innovative   ☐ Writing an outline

☐ Observation   ☐ Talking to others   ☐ Following directions

4. How do you prefer working?

☐ Alone   ☐ With one or two others   ☐ In a group

☐ With an experienced colleague   ☐ In a variety of settings

5. Which learning modality do you prefer?

☐ Auditory   ☐ Visual   ☐ Kinesthetic

Stress Buster Checklist

☐ 1. Use humor—laughter reduces stress.

☐ 2. Ask for and accept help from others.

☐ 3. Learn to accept what you cannot change.

☐ 4. Get enough rest and sleep.

☐ 5. Stay optimistic.

☐ 6. Be flexible.

☐ 7. Balance work and family.

☐ 8. Interface with a network of friends or colleagues when facing a
challenge. Talk it out.

☐ 9. Look at unexpected changes as challenges and opportunities.

☐ 10. Schedule quiet time (reflection time) for yourself every day.

Financial Management

The center director is expected to have the knowledge and skills necessary to provide an appropriate program for children. However, the need for a center director to have an understanding of the financial aspects of the center is often overlooked. The center's program is dependent upon sound financial management. A center's budget directly affects its program and its policy. It is crucial that you develop an understanding of effective financial planning and management.

Subjects & Predicates

Let's look at the ways in which money is equated with program quality. First and most obvious is staffing. Optimal teacher/child ratios mean a safer environment and proper individualized attention for each child.

Appropriate salaries mean lower turnover rates and happier staff. This continuity of care by competent, cheerful people makes for a greater degree of emotional security for the children.

Certainly staff members are more effective and committed in their work when they have adequate assistance in the classrooms; adequate support personnel in the housekeeping, bus driving, and food services departments; satisfactory vacation schedules; and, above all, acceptable salary levels.

Second, budget allotments dictate the quality and quantity of equipment and supplies used throughout the program. Having a variety of teaching materials and appropriate equipment in the classroom helps staff plan and implement stimulating activities in a safe environment, in both outside play areas and indoor space.

Some questions you should consider when establishing a program goal are listed below. They serve as a reminder of the relationship between planning and the budget.

Planning the Commitment of Resources

1. Should this issue be considered?
2. What level of quality do I want?
3. In what ways should this issue be implemented?
4. How much should it cost?

Let's take the purchase of a new piece of equipment for the playground as an example, and apply the above questions to the process.

Considering the Purchase of Playground Equipment

1. Does the center need this piece of equipment? What will it add to the program in the area of children's growth and development? How does the staff feel about it?
2. What should the quality level of this equipment be in terms of state requirements, safety standards, and longevity and repair needs? Naturally, the equipment should be appropriate to the developmental level of the children who will use it.
3. In what ways can the center implement this purchase? Should the complete piece be purchased, or can it be bought in sections? Is fund raising available for this specific purpose, if the center is non-profit or a co-op? Does the playground need to be prepared for the installation of this equipment? If so, a timetable needs to be established and funds allocated for this work.
4. What is a fair price for this piece of equipment? This involves getting bids from vendors based on your specifications, writing a purchase order, and inspecting and approving the merchandise when you receive it.

It is a productive process to use this reflective thinking approach for any area of your work relating to budget.

Staff participation in formulating the budget makes clear to them the goals of the organization. Operating under established budget guidelines is a necessary form of control for the organization.

The organizational arrangement of the child care center determines the specific budgeting methods. If your center is subsidized, such as a United Way agency, you need to determine how much income will be derived from tuition, volunteer help, and in-kind contributions. The deficit, if there is one, will then need to come from community sources. If your organization is a self-supporting operation, clearly the goal is to be able to operate with funds received through tuition. (See Appendix B for sample collection letters.)

Since a quality program costs a great deal, it is often difficult to balance the budget. This is not news to anyone who has run a center. One challenge is having sufficient enrollment. The number of children must exceed the break-even point. To find your break-even point, multiply the number of children by the tuition each pays. The product must equal the total operating expenses. If you are starting a program, it is essential to calculate your break-even point.

Cash flow is critical in operating any business. Simply put, healthy cash flow means income is received in time to pay costs such as salaries and rent. You must project costs over a twelve-month period so that you will know the working capital required to cover these costs.

Steps in Budget Development

The following steps for establishing a center budget are listed in the order in which they occur.

1. Budget guidelines are set at the highest administrative level (board, owner, or administrator) and cover capital, operating costs, salary, and discretionary items.
2. The following individuals initially prepare the various budget components: program budget—center director or program director; food services budget—dietician; accounting budget—comptroller.
3. These individuals negotiate with administration to develop final plans for each component.
4. Administration coordinates and reviews the components.
5. Administration gives final approval.
6. The approved budget is distributed with permission to implement.

Statements showing monthly and cumulative expenditures should be distributed regularly during the year. Methods of reporting on expenditures and all guidelines as to purchasing, petty cash, charge accounts, and supplies should be in writing and on file.

Annual Budget Format

A budget contains two parts. The first is a listing of the main items. The second is a breakdown within each item, justifying the total figure. The following is an example of a simple annual budget, including the breakdown for each main item:

INCOME: $_____

Registration fees _____
Tuition fees _____
Special fees, charges _____
Fund raising (fairs, sales of T-shirts, etc.) _____
Gifts, contributions _____
Loans _____
Miscellaneous _____

EXPENDITURES: $_____

STAFF SERVICES: $_____

Salaries—
    Regular staff _____
    Substitute staff _____
Indirect costs—
    Fringe benefits, payroll, taxes _____
    Consultants _____
    In-service training and information _____
    Memberships _____

SPACE COSTS: $_____

Facility rental _____
Utilities _____
Communications _____
Custodial _____
Maintenance _____
Insurance, building _____

SUPPLIES: $———

Teaching (program)	———
Food	———
Office	———
Housekeeping	———
Maintenance	———
Transportation	———
Other	———

EQUIPMENT: $———

Kitchen	———
Playground	———
Classrooms	———
Office	———
Transport	———
Other	———

OTHER EXPENSES: $———

Publicity, public relations	———
Audit	———
Dues, memberships	———
License fees, permits	———
Printing, postage, mailing	———
Loan payments	———
Uncollectible accounts	———

Maintaining Income

How do you operate a program on only the tuition taken in? It is highly unlikely that you can! Families can afford to pay about 10 percent of their income for child care. This is usually not enough to support a program (especially for infants and toddlers, where staff/child ratios increase costs). The federal child care tax credit is a personal income tax program that subsidizes between 20 and 30 percent of what families pay for your program. Legislative changes in tax credits are constantly under consideration. Keep alert to current allowances.

Some centers offer a sliding fee scale in which tuitions are based on family income. It is difficult to establish criteria and verify income information. Some families resent this method of setting fees. An alternative to a sliding fee scale is to set standard fees and then offer scholarship aid where needed. Often this is a more acceptable approach.

As you work on this challenge, it is essential to make clear your policies on attendance, holidays, and vacation times. If families do not pay during their annual vacation, for example, you must factor this into the fee schedule. It is faulty planning to assume that you will receive income from tuition over a twelve-month period, when in reality a two-week vacation, sick days, and ten holidays are deducted.

If you do not collect tuition when it is due, you will soon be in a cash flow bind. (See Appendix B for sample collection letters.) Set up clear collection policies and monitor the payment records constantly. Keep in mind that to stay in business, enrollment must be maintained well above the break-even point, with utilization kept at over 90 percent for a one-year period. You should aim for a 95 percent utilization rate. Active attention to public relations and offering a variety of quality programs are two ongoing activities that will have a positive effect on enrollment.

Generally speaking, tuition received must be supplemented by some kinds of fund raising, such as selling T-shirts, sponsoring seminars, and hosting book fairs. For example, one center director sold doughnuts and bagels on Fridays. Quality programs and well-planned public relations can lead to donations and in-kind services.

Careful use of supplies and extra attention to staffing patterns are ways to make the most of income received; the child care center stays afloat by paying attention to how every penny is spent.

The Importance of Financial Records

It has been said that a major downfall of managers in any field is the failure to keep complete records. In child care, it is absolutely essential to keep clear, up-to-date accounts of dollars received and dollars spent.

To check yourself, refer to the discussion of record keeping in Chapter 2. Be sure that you are knowledgeable about each item in the section on business management records. Have you made the necessary forms, collected and recorded the needed figures, and devised a practical filing system? Are you aware of tax and other government requirements?

You can find many good record keeping books. Select one that provides space for recording weekly and monthly attendance and fees for each child. Be sure to note fees due and fees received, and any adjustments in fees (document the reason for adjustment). Note the bank account number to make checking on payments easier. Keep financial records in triplicate.

Do not hesitate to hire a bookkeeper and/or an accountant. The cost of this skilled person may keep your center from going under.

Of course you will have a yearly audit of your financial records. In addition, it is imperative that you set up procedures for controlling receipts (particularly for cash payments received), signing of checks, and so on, so that there is little temptation for theft or misuse of funds. Bonding insurance is usually recommended as a wise part of your insurance package. More than one person should be involved in recording monies received and monies spent.

When the records are current, the information needed for decision making to keep the center running is at your fingertips. Periodic reviews of your financial situation will alert you to trouble. A quick response by the administration can mean the difference between success and failure. For example, if your attendance is slipping, with resulting income loss, you will need to put a plan into action to recruit new students.

Important Points in Sound Financial Management
- Thorough record keeping
- Regular review of finances
- Remedial action, where needed

A number of software providers offer information on child care center accounting (full accounting, billing, budgeting, flexible fees, employee payroll, expense reports, and more). An example can be found at:
URL
http://www.zdnet.com/products/stories/reviews/0.4161.2433824.oo.html

Sound financial management can be viewed as the "enabling ingredient" of all the duties you assume. It makes possible the program you are dedicated to provide.

Recommended Reading

Cherry, C., B. Harkness, & K. Kuzma. (1987). *Nursery school and day care management*. Torrance, CA: Lake Publishing Group.

Guide to successful fundraising. (1989). Redmond, WA: Exchange Press.

Managing money: A center director's guidebook. (1998). Redmond, WA: Exchange Press.

Montanari, E.O. (1992). *101 ways to build enrollment in your early childhood program*. St. Paul, MN: Redleaf Press.

On-target marketing: Promotion strategies for child care centers. (1996). Redmond, WA: Exchange Press.

Sciarra, J. & A.G. Dorsey. (1998). *Developing and administering a child care center* (3rd ed.). New York: Delmar Publishers.

Internet Resources

Find reviews of small-business accounting software (QuickBooks, Peachtree, MYOB, etc.) at URL
http://www.zdnet.com/products/stories/reviews/0,4161,2433824,00.html

U.S. Small Business Administration (SBA). (1999). *Child Day-Care Services*. Management and Planning Series Publication MP-30. Business plan, cash flow analysis, financial sources, marketing, operations models, appendixes on state regulatory agencies, licensing, and information resources.
URL http://www.sba.gov/library/pubs/mp-30.doc

Software Providers – A number of software providers offer information on child care center information management software (record keeping, child and parent information, health forms, reports, permission forms, contracts, and so on). Some examples can be found at: URL
http://www.on-qsofttware.com, http://www.childcareadmin.com, http://www.providerware.com, http://www.sba.gov/library/pubs/mp-30.doc, http://www.daycaresoftware.com, http://www.kasksoftware.com, http://www.daycareorganizer.com

Public Relations

Working with Families

It is not unusual to hear early childhood educators comment, "I love my work with the children—but, oh, the parents!" *Beware!* You must keep in mind that child care definitely means working with the family unit if you are to be successful with the child.

Nancy Alexander

The center director is usually the first person to develop a relationship with the family. During the initial meeting with the family, the director expresses the attitudes of the center toward the family (i.e., sets the tone of the center). It is beneficial for you to explain the programs, daily schedules, the center's philosophies concerning discipline and nutrition, tuition policies, and so on.

Equally important, the director must convey a sincere interest in any concerns the families may have. Listen carefully and take notes on how the family feels about the education of their child, discipline, and on their overall expectations of the center. Successful placement of the child in your center means reaching a mutual agreement between the goals of the family and those of the center.

Spend as much time as necessary orienting the family to the routine operations of the center. This will cut down on the amount of anxiety when the time finally arrives for the family to leave their child with the teacher.

Since the child's caregiver will become the ongoing link between the home and the center, it is imperative for you to choose staff members who are secure in their dealings with families and who view themselves as "partners" with the family in the best interest of each child. It is wise to spend some in-service time on family-teacher relationships. The Faculty Manual in Appendix E contains some helpful hints in this area, including a section that carefully explains to staff members the center's policies on communication with families.

Investigate new technologies that will help you create your own web page as well as provide direct communication with families. For example, consider installing cameras in each room that perform Internet communication functions. Families can access the system using a code and see their child in real time. Use of such a tool gives you:

- a competitive edge in the market
- the potential to lower your insurance rate
- help in staff training
- a way to monitor center activities
- an increase in family-teacher communications

Family-Teacher Conferences

For more information on family-teacher conferences, such as the reason for them, necessary preparation, and a suggested format to follow, see Appendix E. It is important to keep a written report on any meeting between staff and families. This keeps communication clear and helps avoid future misunderstandings.

Families sometimes feel anxious when they find themselves having to share their child's affection and loyalty with the teacher. Therefore, family-teacher conferences are more likely to be successful when the teacher approaches the meeting strictly as a teacher and not as a "teacher-parent" figure for the child. The aware teacher *does not* let a situation involving any type of rivalry develop.

Keep in mind that families may also be anxious about the separation from their child and the criticism that often results from cultural attitudes. Because anxiety can interfere with the smooth flow of communication between families and the teacher, it is important for the teacher to put any feelings of inadequacy to rest.

The director usually does not need to be involved in family-teacher conferences unless a serious problem arises. If you do have to become involved, however, the following suggestions may be helpful:

Suggestions for Conferences with Families

- Do what you can to alleviate the anxiety of the family members—remember to emphasize the child's positive qualities.
- Express appreciation for the family's participation.
- Describe what you see happening with the child, without using labels.
- Ask families if they have observed similar incidents at home (listening skills are particularly helpful at this time).
- Have anecdotal records available (any data that might be helpful in talking with the family).
- End the conference with a specific plan of action and a date for a follow-up meeting, if necessary.

Avoid becoming a "therapist" for families. You are trained in early childhood development and the education of young children; therefore, sharing this knowledge with families is appropriate and helpful. However, be aware of the need to limit your involvement in serious family issues to a warm, caring attitude. Provide the troubled family with helpful information such as lists of professional agencies, clinics, and other professionals qualified to assist them with their problems.

Family Education

Encourage families to enrich their understanding of early childhood education, the development of their own child, and behavior modification techniques. They can learn much by observing groups of children in the center classrooms. Invite them to make a series of visits to the center at different times of the day so that they can observe a variety of activities.

The center should reach out to families and provide meaningful programs that address common family concerns, such as:

- Appropriate toys for children
- Time-saving techniques for nutrition and meal preparation
- Where to obtain medical and legal advice
- Issues of child rearing, step-parenting, discipline, and how children learn

Vary the format of your meetings (informational, workshop, or even using an outdoor location to provide a change of environment).

Families want their children to succeed academically, but often have misunderstandings about how young children learn. Below are some suggested topics to use in informal, small group situations to help families develop appropriate expectations for their children.

Topics Suitable for Small Group Meetings

- Discuss how to encourage a child to use words and sentences. For example, how to phrase a question in a way that requires a verbal response.
- Demonstrate how to give specific instructions to a child and to observe how the child follows them.
- Discuss the importance of reading to the child on a regular basis, listening to music, and taking trips to interesting places, such as the zoo. Discuss how developing the ability to read is related to experiences.
- Discuss the importance of a healthy self-image and ways to help the child develop positive self-esteem.
- Discuss the importance of physical activity to the health and neurological development of children.
- Talk about the development of self-discipline.
- Discuss how self-reliance and independence help a child.

Family Involvement

Learn the names of family members so that you can greet them warmly when you see them. Provide a place where they can gather. You can often add a special touch by making coffee or cold drinks available to them.

When planning family programs, always be sure to send a written invitation. You can make it even more personal if you ask their child to decorate it. (This also makes it more likely to be brought to someone's attention.) Try to extend a personal invitation when you see the families; you may want to make telephone calls as well.

Work closely with classroom teachers as you develop programs. Based on teacher interactions with families, you can personalize activities to meet real needs. Pertinent programs are successful programs.

Organize a committee made up of family members or set up a system of "room helpers" to help plan programs, classroom parties, and outings. You might want to develop a form for families to fill out listing their special interests, skills, or hobbies, so that you will know whom to call for special help.

Encourage staff members to keep open lines of communication between themselves and families by sending home notices about special class happenings. Families need to hear about the things that are going well—not just the challenges. (Notes are not recommended for discussing problems.)

You may find that some families would be interested in coming to in-service programs developed for staff. Invite them—it will provide a new dimension in learning for families and staff members to share.

The following are additional approaches often used at child care centers to promote family-center interaction:

- Develop a lending library of reference materials, such as books, magazines, and journal articles, that pertain to family issues.
- Offer a lending library of toys, educational materials, and dramatic play items for children and families.
- Ask families to contribute to the center newsletter. For example, there could even be a "swap" column of used children's clothing, furniture, and toys.

- Ask families with creative skills to share in bulletin board preparation and theme selection.

Families who are secure in their choice of child care are essential to a successful center. Security comes with time as trust develops between families and the center. It is enhanced when families are well informed and are involved in the program. A happy and secure home-center connection increases the potential for the child to have a pleasant and successful child care experience.

Working with the Community

Your success as a center director will depend to a large extent on your ability to interact with the community. Of course, you must cooperate with licensing agents, health inspectors, and fire marshals just to maintain your ability to operate. Interacting with outside agencies, however, goes far beyond day-to-day operation and into the framework of the community. Your ability to interface with others can help you increase your visibility and make a place in the community.

Establish a relationship with area colleges and training institutes. Get to know the professors and attend appropriate meetings and seminars offered by these schools of education. Send your publications to key persons in the early childhood department. Offer your center as a placement for student training.

An example of such an institute is the Center for Career Development in Early Care and Education at Wheelock College in Boston, Massachusetts. This center is involved in a partnership with other national organizations and government policy makers. Staying in contact with institutes like this one keeps you on the forefront of national, state, and local issues that affect your center in both areas of business and curriculum.

Join the Chamber of Commerce and any other area professional organizations that pertain to your business. Let the appropriate persons know that you are available to speak at Rotary Clubs, Lions Clubs, garden clubs, and so on. Topics might include "The Value of Child Care," "How to Select Quality Care," "Latchkey Children," or any other topic that you feel comfortable talking about.

Be available to serve as a judge for science fairs, carnivals, and other community projects. Also, serving as a panelist on career day in area high schools is an effective way of maintaining visibility and showing your interest in the development of children.

When local organizations ask for support in community projects, try to participate. It is more effective if you can involve the children and staff in your center. For example, you might sponsor a carnival, with all proceeds going to United Way or some other organization. The staff and children can select, build, and maintain booths for the carnival. What a great story for the local paper!

Maintaining public relations requires a great deal of your time but is well worth the effort. Utilize the techniques of time management described in Chapter 2. Delegate work to others when possible so that you can properly focus on the public relations aspect of your job. People remember those in the community who are ready to help others. Being an active community member can help you maintain and increase your current enrollment. Community involvement pays off when you need community support.

Development of Publications

As noted in Chapter 3, publicity is part of a center's budget. Clearly stated information, attractively and creatively presented in print and properly distributed, is a major avenue for keeping enrollment at the optimum level. Check your budget line for publicity to be sure your figure is realistic.

Brochures

Brochures can be classified into two types. The first type is the brochure that the center will use over a long period of time. This type of brochure should be printed on quality paper, and its design and color should be well thought out. Its purpose is to "catch the eye" of families seeking quality child care and to provide information of a general nature about your center. This, of course, is also the more expensive type of brochure.

Investigate at least *three* printing companies. Check on the extent of the service they provide. (Do they develop logos and business cards? What is the timeframe for delivery?) Ask to preview samples of their work and compare price and quality.

After you select a printer, prepare the following information about your center in double-spaced, typed format:

- Name
- Logo, if already designed
- Address (perhaps a simple map, too)
- Phone number(s)
- Years in business and some general staff information
- Hours of child care (for example, full day: 6:30 a.m. to 6:30 p.m., after school: 3 p.m.to 6:30 p.m.)
- Services provided

For the last item, you might want to write a brief description of each of your programs. For example:

After school program: a program tailored to meet the needs of the older child. A trained gym instructor provides the opportunity for fun and movement after a day in school. Tutors are available to help with homework, and an arts/crafts program is offered as well. A nutritious snack is included. Transportation from the school to the center can also be provided.

Take your information to the printer and select a quality paper. The paper should be able to withstand a lot of handling and convey the feeling that the center is successful. Usually, the finished product is folded so that it can easily fit into a purse or pocket. Naturally, what appears on the top fold should be eye catching and make the reader want to look further into the brochure. The printer should be able to assist you in selecting size, color, print type, logo placement, and the use of photos or drawings.

An effective brochure should provide enough information to evoke interest in your center, give a sense of the center's philosophy, and convey an image of high quality care for children.

The second type of brochure contains information that will have to be updated from time to time, such as tuition costs and special fees. Because it will have to be revised often, you should select a less expensive format. For example, the paper can be of a much lesser quality (and expense), and it can be printed in black and white, which will also reduce the cost of printing it.

In addition to this second brochure, you might want to provide a family handbook similar to the manual for new staff members (see Appendix E). The handbook would most likely contain:

- A welcome letter
- Calendar
- Center policies and procedures
- Field trip information
- Drop-off and pick-up procedures

You might also want to place the brochure that contains tuition information inside the front cover.

Be sure your material is carefully proofread. Printed information conveys a definite message about your center. Misspellings and poor grammar project a negative and unprofessional image.

Newsletters

Newsletters are an excellent vehicle for providing information and creating interest in the center's programs and activities. Include a monthly calendar of events and perhaps a birthday list. If the calendar is placed on a separate page (perhaps page one), families can post it in their homes as a reminder.

The newsletter should contain information that families will want to read about, such as what is happening in their child's classroom. Ask your staff members to contribute short stories and descriptions of current and upcoming events or activities. As you read the sample newsletter in Appendix A, you will note that different staff members have different writing styles. This adds to the interest and variety of the newsletter. You will also notice that *families* are addressed throughout the sample newsletter (family-teacher conferences, family volunteer information, family involvement, family meeting information, and billing information).

From time to time, check your method of distributing the newsletter to make sure families are receiving it. Don't be discouraged if you find that it is not always read. Most families do read it, but some never will.

As mentioned earlier, to create more family interest in the newsletter, you may want to incorporate a regular column written by family members. This is an issue that can be addressed by a committee comprised of family members. You may find that families will offer to help with the typing, printing, and distribution of notices and newsletters. (See sample newsletters in Appendix A.)

Recommended Reading

Aronson, S., S. Bradley, S. Louchheim, D. Mancuso, & E. Unguary. (1997). *Model child care health policies*. Washington, DC: National Association for the Education of Young Children (NAEYC).

Brazelton, T.B. & S.I. Greenspan. (2000). *The irreducible needs of children: What every child must have to grow, learn, and flourish*. Cambridge, MA: Perseus Books.

Brazelton, T.B. (1994). *Touchpoints: Your child's emotional and behavioral development*. Cambridge, MA: Perseus Books.

Couchenour, D. & K. Chrisman. (1999). *Families, schools, and communication: Working together for young children*. Albany, NY: Delmar.

Mogharreban, C. & S. Branscum. (2000). Educare: Community collaboration for school readiness. *Dimesions of Early Childhood,* 28(1, Winter).

On-target marketing: Promotion strategies for child care centers. (1996). Redmond, WA: Exchange Press.

Ramey, C.T. & S.L. Ramey. (1999). *Right from birth: Building your child's foundation for life*. New York: Goddard Press, Inc.

Reisser, P.C. & J.C. Dobson. (1997). *The focus on the family complete book of baby and childcare*. Carol Stream, IL: Tyndale House Publishers.

Satter, E. (2000). *Child of mine: Feeding with love and good sense*. Palo Alto, CA: Bull Publishing Company.

Schiller, P. & T. Bryant. (1998). *The values book*. Beltsville, MD: Gryphon House.

Schiller, P. (1999). *Start smart: Building brain power in the early years*. Beltsville, MD: Gryphon House.

Swick, K.J. (1991). *Teacher-parent partnerships to enhance school success in early childhood programs*. Published by the Southern Early Childhood Association division for the Development and the National Education Association (formerly Southern Association of Children Under Six). Available through SECA: URL http://www.seca50.org.resourcesBOOKS2.html

Van De Zande, I. (1993). *1, 2, 3...The toddler years: A practical guide for parents and caregivers*. Santa Cruz, CA: Santa Cruz Toddler Center.

Resources

Center for Career Development in Early Care and Education
Wheelock College
200 The Riverway
Boston, MA 02215
(617) 734-5200
http://ericps.crc.uiuc.edu/ccdece/ccdece.html

Software Management Packages

DATACARE
R.P.M. Software (800) 252-4776
http://www.rpmwebworx.com/rpmsoft/daycare.html

Childcare Administrator 2000
http://www.childcareadmin.com/featmain.htm

DayCare Information Systems Pro 2000 for Centers
SDS Software Solutions
2079 Rifle River Trail
West Branch, MI 48661
(800) 486-6960
http://www.daycaresoftware.com/32bit/2000/centerbased/dayc.../default_main.ht

Internet Resources

Owners, Directors, and Childcare Professionals. Internet tools.
URL http://www.watchmegrow.com/wmgdirector.htm

Viewing Systems for Child Care
URL www.parent-view.com, www.kinderview.com

National Resource Center for Health and Safety in Child Care.
URL http://www.nrc.uchsc.edu

I Am Your Child.
URL http://www.iamyourchild.org

Personnel Policies and Procedures

5

Policies on Staff Selection

The availability of trained child care workers varies. In areas near training institutions such as junior or community colleges, the number of competent caregivers probably is highest. What can the director do to ensure adequate, quality staffing of the center? There are three components of a staff selection policy. First, you must make a decision about the level of education and experience that will be required of incoming staff. Will you use the minimum standards required by law, or do you expect more? (See Appendix D for descriptions of qualifications for teachers and teacher's aides.)

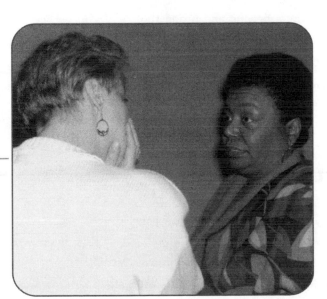

Subjects & Predicates

The second aspect of staff selection is planning and providing a pertinent training program. Realistically, it is not always possible to find the "ideal" person, so you should look for certain basic traits and plan an in-service training program geared to the growth and development of staff. When selecting persons who will be responsible for the children, select people who like themselves and enjoy being with children. Since everyone has strengths and weaknesses, try to add staff with strengths needed to balance the existing staff. For example, if you are hiring a second caregiver for the four-year-old classroom and the existing caregiver is skilled at developing math and science activities, try to find someone who enjoys music, art, and drama. At least one of the two teachers should be skilled in classroom management. The best-laid plans will go awry if the room is chaotic. (Further information on training is provided later in this chapter.)

The third component of staff selection is deciding who will be involved in the hiring process. Perhaps it will be only one person—you, the director. However, in large centers or those where a participatory style of management is favored, other staff may take part.

If you have head teachers or supervisors of different age levels in your center, you could invite them to list the skills they think the person to be hired needs. They can also talk with the applicant at some time during the interview and provide input to you. This added input will not only help you make a decision, but will also give your staff the feeling of belonging, training in supervisory skills, and a personal interest in helping to orient the new staff person once he or she is hired. Of course, the effectiveness of this second approach will depend on the level of competency of the supervisors or head teachers.

Additionally, the director is responsible for interviewing and hiring the support staff. Even though these people generally are not directly responsible for children, they should enjoy being around children. (See Appendix D for descriptions of qualifications for food service personnel, assistants, and custodians.)

Interviewing and Selecting Staff

Preparing for interviews is one of the keys to successful staffing of your center. Know the questions you want to ask. Write them down beforehand, unobtrusively check them off as you ask them, and make short notes of the applicant's answers. If you are interviewing several candidates, this will help you organize your information on each person.

Be aware of the kinds of questions you are allowed to ask under the law and those that are not allowed, such as marital status and number of children. Have an attorney check your employment application form to be sure it is legally correct. See Sample Employment Application on page 89 for a sample form that you can adapt to your specific needs.

As mentioned earlier, including staff in the interview process is a technique that builds a sense of community for both the applicant and staff members. If you are going to include staff in the interview, make sure you have arranged for their classrooms to be covered and that you have notified them of their participation early enough to allow them time to prepare.

Many organizations find it useful to use a three-stage interview process. The first stage is used to determine compatibility. It provides an opportunity to inform the applicant of your expectations and to match those expectations to the applicant's expectations.

Ask the applicant to fill out the application form prior to the interview. Review the information on the form before you begin stage one of the interview process. Provide a short article on child development for the applicant to read while you are reviewing the application. Be sure to discuss the article in stage one of the interview. You will learn a lot about your candidate based on whether she reads the article or not.

During the interview, phrase your questions so that they require full answers rather than a yes or no answer. An effective technique is to pose hypothetical scenarios and ask the candidates how they would handle the situations. Ask applicants to expand on the solutions they choose.

It is important to discover the applicants' attitudes toward children and her or his understanding of child development—how children learn, how to help children develop pro-social behaviors, the caregiver's role in helping children grow and develop, and the applicant's understanding of the developmental characteristics of the age group in which she or he will be working.

You also want to learn about the applicants' attitudes toward other co-workers, such as sharing ideas and materials. Questions you might ask include:
- What do you consider "professional" behavior?
- What are some challenges you have encountered in the past involving staff?

How does the applicant feel about working with families? You might ask:

- What success and what difficulties have you had in this area?
- How do you feel about working with families? Why?
- How do you feel about family members visiting the classroom?

You may also want to ask the applicant these questions: What are your career goals, both immediate and long range? How do you feel about in-service training?

Stage two of the interview process is a tour of the building. During this phase, you will want to watch the applicants' interactions with staff and children. Does she or he walk all the way into the classroom? When the candidate speaks to children, does she or he stoop to make eye contact with the child? Does she or he smile at other staff and speak to them when appropriate? Does she or he seem curious about lesson plans, curriculum, and materials?

If stage one and stage two have gone well and you feel this applicant is a viable candidate for the position, move on to stage three. However, if you do not feel the match is acceptable, this is the time to exit the interview by sending the applicant on her or his way.

During stage three, the interview should include only yourself and the applicant. Go over the job description, hours of work, pay, benefits offered, and the start date of employment. Clearly state any probationary aspects of the job. In most other businesses salary is not discussed during the initial interview. However, it is usually a part of the child care interview. Give the applicant the time frame for making a decision and notification of hire.

Applicants need to be fully aware of the job requirements and the working environment. An effective strategy for accomplishing this is to arrange for the applicant to visit a classroom and for the teacher of that class to be available to spend some time talking with the applicant.

Naturally, you must fully address the applicants' questions. Be realistic when you describe the job responsibilities, including the both positive and negative aspects. If you have established core values for your center, you will want to go over these with the applicant.

By way of a summary, here is a suggested outline for the interview process:

Steps in Interviewing

Beforehand

- Write down a list of questions, leaving space for your notes.
- Set a date and time for the interview to take place. Be generous with the time allowance and inform the applicant of the length of the interview.
- Make arrangements for others on staff to be involved.

At Interview Time/Stage One

- Greet the applicant, and ask her or him to fill out the application form. (See Sample Employment Application on page 89.)
- Give the applicant a child development article to read while you go over his or her application.
- Put the applicant at ease. Then ask and answer questions while taking notes. Pay attention to the applicant's compatibility to the position and to the center as a whole.

Stage Two

- Give the applicant a tour of the facility. Pay attention to his or her interactions with the staff and children.

Stage Three

- Exit applicants that do not match your expectations.
  Or, if the applicant appears to be a match:
- Make sure the applicant visits a classroom and talks with a staff person.
- Meet again with the applicant so he or she can ask final questions and have a discussion.
- Discuss benefit packages and salary.

Afterwards

- Check references and check for any criminal records.
- Discuss the applicant's interview with participating staff members. Consider their recommendations.

Once a decision has been reached, notify all applicants—both the successful candidate and the others. Send the chosen candidate a letter offering employment, which should include the position title, salary, and an appointment date to begin the orientation process. Request a written acceptance by the candidate.

Make an announcement regarding the hiring of the new employee to all staff members, and send a copy to the new person as well. Give specific information—well-informed staff will feel a sense of community.

Orientation/Training Procedures

Solid staff orientation and training requires both time and money, but it is a worthwhile expense in the long run. Staff who understand their job expectations and who are trained in classroom procedures make a smoother transition into the classroom and also have a tendency to stay with the job longer. Trained employees are also less likely to need assistance after they are on the job.

Begin the orientation by discussing each item in the Employee Packet (see Appendix C) with the new employee. Then ask the employee to sign the statement of acceptance of policies and conditions for employment (see Employee Agreement form on page 90) and place it in the individual's personnel file. Give the employee a copy of the standards of your regulatory agency and point out the section on Personnel. Provide a copy of the Faculty Manual (see Appendix E), paying particular attention to the section on policies and procedures. Be sure your expectations are clear on the following:

- Calling in if unable to be at work
- Signing in
- Daily schedules and routines
- Naptime
- Staff phone privileges/messages
- Probationary status
- Fire drill procedures
- Emergency medical procedures
- Lesson plans
- Release of children from center
- Staff break times

See that the employee completes all the necessary paperwork, including:

- W-2 Form
- Health statement from physician

- Any statements needing signatures as required by regulatory agencies

You should take the new employee on a tour of the facility, including:
- Adult restrooms
- Location of posted fire evacuation exits, fire extinguisher, and alarm system
- First aid supplies
- Staff supplies and equipment
- Staff workroom and rest area
- Staff library
- Staff bulletin board
- Files for staff use
- Areas for special activities (gym, music, cafeteria)
- Outside play areas

Introduce the new employee to the general staff and his or her supervisor, and in particular to the staff member appointed to assist in the orientation/training. Have the new employee visit a classroom similar to the one where she or he will be working. Give her or him selected materials to read that are relevant to the position, a place in which to read the materials, and time with the supervisor to ask any questions about the materials. Plan some time for observing and assisting the new employee during the orientation and training. At the conclusion of the orientation/training, ask the employee to sign the initial orientation form (see sample on page 91) to indicate that she or he has completed the orientation/training.

Subject & Predicates

In order to allow time for orientation and training, place the employee on the payroll effective one day before the actual start of work for nursery and kindergarten caregivers, and three days before for infant and toddler caregivers.

Probationary Procedures

Observation and evaluation of the new employee during the probationary period is an important part of the staff selection process. Most probationary periods range from two to three months. An informal meeting with the supervisor, the program manager, and the new employee should take place after the first two weeks of employment. A formal review should be held at the conclusion of the first month. Until this period has been successfully completed, the employee is on a trial basis and is not truly part of the staff.

During the candidate's probation, observe him or her on a regular basis at different times of the day, and during a variety of activities. Use a printed list and make written notes with the date, time, and name of the evaluator. *The importance of documentation cannot be stressed enough when dealing with staff.*

Nancy Alexander

THE PRACTICAL GUIDE TO QUALITY CHILD CARE

See the Classroom Teacher—Evaluation During Probation form (page 92) and Classroom Assistant—Probation Checklist (page 93) for sample listings of areas to evaluate when observing a probationary classroom teacher or classroom assistant. Be sure to read each question thoroughly and answer with enough information to document your observations. This information will help you have meaningful conferences with your staff. You should utilize these checklists at approximately the sixth week of employment. This gives the staff member time to adjust to the environment before being evaluated, and allows enough time to make recommended changes before the end of the probationary period.

At a midpoint in the probationary period, have a meeting with the new staff member and go over your observations. Include some written goals and objectives. In addition, add any goals that the new employee feels are important.

Be very clear about any expectations for changes in performance that you feel are necessary for this person to successfully complete the trial period. For example, if a person has been late too often, instead of saying, "We need you to be here on time in the morning," say, "If you are late again without an acceptable reason, you will not pass your probationary period."

If there is a problem, this is the time to make your expectations known and to provide an opportunity for the individual to understand and get the assistance needed to make the required changes. Without this activity on your part, probation is of little value in the hiring process.

Both the evaluator and the staff person should sign the evaluation and listing of goals and objectives. If necessary, set a date to meet again. Shortly before the end of the probationary period, meet once again to determine the employee's outcome. If the employee is successful, congratulations are in order. Make an announcement to all staff and record this information in the individual's personnel file.

If you have decided that the candidate, while given every opportunity to succeed, is not able to do the job at an acceptable level, you need to point out specific reasons for your decision. This is usually difficult, but often the candidate has the self-awareness that she or he is not a match for the position. Ideally, try to point out the strengths that you have observed, and if the person is receptive, suggest areas of employment where these strengths might be utilized. Keep in mind that your responsibility is to provide the best possible care for the children enrolled at the center, and this sometimes means terminating an employee.

In-Service Training

To implement the stated philosophy and goals of the center, meet the needs of your staff to grow professionally, and comply with regulations that mandate training, it is imperative that you provide a high quality, ongoing program of in-service training.

When planning in-service training, attempt to make the programs relevant to the individual needs of your staff. However, keep in mind that the ultimate goal of in-service training is to facilitate implementing the objectives and goals of the program outlined to families and staff. Some suggested topics for in-service training are provided in the form Ideas for In-Service Programs on page 94.

The person responsible for planning in-service training is usually the center director. However, if there is a program director or manager on staff, this would be his or her job.

How do you begin planning in-service training? Become familiar with the goals of the center. Keep them in mind as you observe the daily routines throughout the center. Evaluate the performance of the staff in relation to what you have defined as your philosophy. For instance, do you say you have a developmentally based curriculum? If so, are the kinds of activities being planned appropriate to the levels of development of the children in the group? Is the teacher familiar with the developmental milestones of young children? Can each child have some measures of success with each activity? Does the activity allow for the individual differences within the group?

Ideas for training needs can come from information you gain about new staff during the interview process. The first step in the new employee's training begins with his or her orientation.

An important part of an in-service plan is for staff to self evaluate themselves, with the opportunity for them to request specific training.

Training should facilitate job change within the center organization, and help the trainee meet her or his career goals.

Be specific about the objectives for each training session. Clearly show the employee the steps he or she should take to achieve the desired results. The objectives should be realistic and measurable so that as the trainee tries out the suggestions, she or he can feel a sense of accomplishment. In other words, show how to put the theory into practice. Make sure to keep the environment of the training session nonjudgmental.

Customize the sessions to the participants and invite staff to whom the session content is relevant. The following are some questions you should ask yourself:

- Who should be trained?
- How should this training be done?
- Why is it necessary?
- What will be learned?

Following each training session, ask the participants to evaluate the program using a form such the Training Session Evaluation on page 95. Use their evaluations to improve your in-service training.

Classroom assistants are a valuable part of a busy center's staff. Therefore, you should also include them in the same training sessions for the following reasons:

1. They can learn to measure up to the center's standards for performance and satisfy their need for personal growth on the job.
2. Dissatisfaction, complaints, absenteeism, and turnover can be greatly reduced when employees experience the satisfaction associated with a sense of achievement and the knowledge that they are developing their inherent capabilities.
3. As employees respond to continued training, they can progressively increase their value to the organization and thus prepare themselves for promotion.
4. Continued training can help employees develop their ability to learn and adapt to new methods.

When developing in-service training for classroom assistants, know your objectives and have a clear view of the classroom environment and the behavior you expect of the assistants. Write it all down.

Break down the assistant's job into individual job functions. Prioritize the list of job functions and create a flexible schedule for accomplishing them. Use this schedule in the training sessions.

Schedule regular meetings with classroom assistants to discuss and document progress, and to see if further training is needed or requested.

A wise director understands that the level of competency of the center staff is an indicator of the quality of the programs offered. Planning and carrying out effective staff training, therefore, should have high priority among the responsibilities of a director.

Staff Evaluation

An example of a staff evaluation form is on page 96 (Sample Employee Performance Review). Adapt the form to your particular needs and be sure that every member of your staff has a copy. You should have an ongoing schedule for staff evaluations. You might consider developing a form that staff members could use for self-evaluations. A teacher or director can use the evaluation form on page 97 when viewing a videotape of a day in the classroom.

The purpose of staff evaluations is to improve the program. To be meaningful, an evaluation must be done with a fair, caring, and responsive attitude. When having a conference following an evaluation, begin by identifying the strengths of the employee. If there is an apparent weakness, provide him or her with concrete ideas for possible improvement.

Substitute Staff

Young children need the security that comes from being with the same caregiver each day. However, this is not always possible. Be sure that needed information is available in each room so that even a last-minute staff replacement can function well. See the Room Schedule form on page 98 for an example of an activity form that teachers can post on their classroom door so the substitute can refer to it to determine what activity comes next in the children's schedule. You should also make available special medical information on children in the class (see Sample Medical Information on page 99). In addition, you might also provide the procedures section of the Faculty Manual (see Appendix E) as well as any other information pertinent to your particular program.

It would also be helpful to post a list of emergency numbers near the telephone, as well as specific instructions for using the center's telephone system. Be sure to introduce the substitute to coworkers so that she or he will have a source for answers to any questions that might come up.

Recommended Reading

Albrecht, K. & L. Miller. (2000). *Innovations: The comprehensive infant curriculum.* Beltsville, MD: Gryphon House.

Albrecht, K. & L. Miller. (2000). *Innovations: The comprehensive toddler curriculum.* Beltsville, MD: Gryphon House.

Alexander, N. (2000). *Workshops that work!* Beltsville, MD: Gryphon House.

American Psychological Association, Inc. (1967). *Casebook of ethical standards of psychologists.* Washington, DC: American Psychological Association, Inc.

Brazelton, T.B. (1994). *Touchpoints: Your child's emotional and behavioral development.* Cambridge, MA: Perseus Books.

Bronson, M.B. (2000). Recognizing and supporting the development of self-regulation in young children. *Young Children,* 55(2, March), 33-37.

Cartwright, S. (1998). Caregivers of quality: Essential attributes of teachers of young children. *Child Care Information Exchange,* March/April (order #12006).

Cartwright, S. (1999). What makes good preschool teachers? *Young Children,* 54(4, July), 4-7.

Da Ros, D.A. & B.A. Kovach. (1998). Assisting toddlers and caregivers during conflict resolutions: Interactions that promote socialization. *Childhood Education,* 75(1, Fall), 1 30.

Dodge, D.T. & L.J. Colker. (1992). *The creative curriculum.* Washington, DC: Teaching Strategies.

Dombro, A.L., L.J. Colker, & D.T. Dodge. (1999). *The creative curriculum for infants and toddlers*. Washington, DC: Teaching Strategies.

Goleman, D. (1995). *Emotional intelligence*. New York: Bantam Books.

Haas-Foletta, K. & M. Cogley. (1990). *School-age ideas and activities for after school programs*. Nashville, TN: School Age Notes.

MacDonald, S. (1997). *Portfolio and its use: A road map for assessment*. Beltsville, MD: Gryphon House.

Neugebauer, R. (1978). Staff selection. *Child Care Information Exchange*. Redmond, WA. Reprint #7.

Neugebauer, R. & B. Neugebauer. (1998). *The art of leadership: Managing early childhood organizations*. Redmond, WA: Exchange Press.

Schiller, P. (1986). *The school-home connection*. Columbus, OH: SRA.

Schiller, P. (1997). *Practices in the early childhood classroom*. Columbus, Ohio: SRA.

Sample Employment Application

Date _____ Social Security # _____

Name _____

Address _____
    Street   City   State   Zip

Are you 18 years or older? _____

Do you have a high school diploma? _____

Name of School _____

Location _____

Please list any education beyond the high school level:

Name of Institution   Location   Degree Earned
_____

Please list any experience or special training you have had that you feel qualifies you for this position:

_____

_____

_____

Do you have any physical disabilities that would hinder you from lifting a small child? If yes, please explain.

_____

_____

_____

Please give your reasons for seeking a position in early childhood education.

_____

_____

_____

Please list any hobbies or special interests: _____

_____

Previous Employment History:

Company   Beg. Date   End Date   Beg. Salary   End Salary
_____

_____

Reason for leaving most recent job: _____

List the names and addresses of three character references:

    Name   Address

1) _____

2) _____

3) _____

Telephone # (_____) _____

Employee Agreement

I have read the standards and guidelines for employment, and I am in accord with the stated policies and conditions for employment at

_____

Name of Center

Date _____

_____

Employee signature

_____ (Center name) does not and will not discriminate against employees on the basis of race, color, religion, sex, age, national or ethnic origin.

ORIENTATION HISTORY

Name: _____

Position/title: _____

Date of hire: _____

Initial orientation: Date: _____ Time: _____

Employee signature: _____

Follow-up Orientation Sessions:

_____
Date   Time   Signature

Sample Personnel Orientation

Classroom Teacher—Evaluation During Probation

Name _____ Date _____

Answer each question completely, with examples when possible.

Are the teacher's personal qualities appropriate for the child care center? For example, is she or he reliable, punctual? Does he or she dress appropriately?

What kind of response does she or he give to your directions? To constructive criticism?

Does she or he use appropriate communication skills with the children? Parents? Peers? Supervisor?

Does she or he have a sense of humor?

Is she or he flexible, adaptable?

Is she or he receptive to new ideas? To learning new skills?

Does she or he show initiative? Responsibility? Has she or he become familiar with school policy?

How does he or she handle the paperwork?

Are classroom management skills utilized? Is the classroom neat and attractive? Are the children encouraged to use self-control? Are the children encouraged to participate? Is the teacher concerned about the safety of each child?

Is the classroom program developmentally appropriate? Is the teacher aware of individual needs? Is the teacher well prepared? Does she or he speak clearly and in a pleasant tone?

Goals and Objectives:

Signatures:

_____   _____
Staff Member   Evaluator

Name _____ Date _____

Answer each question completely, with examples when possible.

1. Does she or he show willingness to learn about early childhood education? Is she or he willing to attend workshops and actively participate in them? Does she or he accept and use constructive criticism?

2. Is she or he punctual and conscientious? Is she or he flexible, able to adapt to sudden changes in schedule? Does she or he have the energy level necessary for this work?

3. Does she or he participate in planning programs? Does she or he help implement the plans? Does she or he help create teaching aids and plan activities?

4. Does she or he keep the classroom tidy? Does she or he encourage children to participate in cleaning up?

5. Does she or he make families feel welcome but refrain from answering questions concerning children's behavior and progress?

6. Does she or he have rapport with the children? Does she or he handle behavior problems in an appropriate manner? Does she or he accept all the children in the group? Are the children able to express unhappiness and anger and get comfort and help from this caregiver?

7. Is she or he cognizant of the health and safety needs of the children?

8. Does she or he gossip with other staff? Does she or he hide personal problems while with the children? Does she or he maintain confidentiality concerning children and their families?

Goals and Objectives:

   Signatures:

_____   _____
          Staff Member   Evaluator

Classroom Assistant—Probation Checklist

Ideas for In-Service Programs

1. Working with children

   Child growth and development

   Curriculum planning for age levels or departments

   - Brain-based learning
   - Encouragement of children to make choices
   - How to manage learning centers
   - Outdoor teaching opportunities
   - Importance of motor program—indoors and outdoors

   Classroom management

   - Specific ways to handle transition
   - Circle or group time
   - Snack time
   - Naptime
   - How to talk to children
   - Philosophy of discipline/guidance
   - Techniques for handling troubling behaviors

   How to observe and describe children

   Physical environment

   - How to facilitate program goals indoors
   - How to set up learning centers
   - Art equipment selection
   - Health and hygiene
   - Safety, CPR, Red Cross training
   - Environmental influences on early brain development
   - Outdoor equipment

2. Working with families

   How to make families feel comfortable in the center

   Understanding family concerns

   Ways to involve families in the life of the center

   How to be effective in a family-teacher conference

   How to make a home visit

   Bulletin board for families

   Newsletters for families

3. Working with peers and supervisors

   Team teaching

   Professionalism in peer interactions

   Career planning

   How to facilitate change in the workplace

   Effective communication—written and oral

   Supervisory skills

   Problem-solving techniques

   Assertiveness training

Please rate the following items from 1 [not at all] to 4 [very well] by circling the appropriate number.

1. The objectives of this session were clearly communicated.

    1   2   3   4

2. The instructor's manner and presentation helped you to meet the objectives.

    1   2   3   4

3. Opportunity was provided for questions, comments, discussions, or other helpful participation.

    1   2   3   4

4. Content was comprehensive and pertinent to the objectives.

    1   2   3   4

5. Audio-visuals and handouts were valuable supplements.

    1   2   3   4

Suggestions for improvement:

_____

_____

_____

Suggestions for next in-service session:

_____

_____

_____

Training Session Evaluation

Sample Employee Performance Review

Name _____

Employee ID Number _____

Dept/Position _____

Please rate the employee in the following areas:

Job knowledge: ☐ outstanding ☐ good ☐ satisfactory ☐ unsatisfactory

Quality of work: ☐ outstanding ☐ good ☐ satisfactory ☐ unsatisfactory

Dependability: ☐ outstanding ☐ good ☐ satisfactory ☐ unsatisfactory

Interpersonal skills: ☐ outstanding ☐ good ☐ satisfactory ☐ unsatisfactory

Adaptability: ☐ outstanding ☐ good ☐ satisfactory ☐ unsatisfactory

What are the strong points of this employee?

_____

_____

What areas of the employee's performance need improvement?

_____

_____

What action do you and the employee intend to take in the next twelve months to increase her or his effectiveness:

_____

_____

Overall evaluation of employee's performance:

☐ outstanding ☐ good ☐ satisfactory ☐ unsatisfactory

Present Weekly Salary $_____

Salary Recommendation $_____

Date review completed: _____ Date of follow-up review: _____

Comments:

Activities taking place: _____

Noise level of group: _____

Directions by the teacher: ☐ clear   ☐ unclear

Voice tone of the teacher: _____

Are "choices" given appropriately? _____

Attitudes of children: ☐ polite   ☐ friendly   ☐ rude

Attitudes of adults: ☐ polite   ☐ friendly   ☐ rude

Are rules clearly given (by teacher)? _____

How are questions phrased (by teacher)? _____

Do questions evoke children's use of language? _____

How does the teacher respond when the answer is not what she/he is looking for?

_____

Does the teacher ever respond with "no" to a child's answer?

_____

How does the teacher bring a child into the conversation or get a child's attention if

he/she withdraws? _____

How many times did the children and teacher laugh during this session?

_____

Did the teacher offer any personal information to children during this session?

_____

If so, what was the response of the children? _____

Did every child find something of interest during the activities?

_____

Did any activity involve every child during this session? _____

What has been gained by this process of evaluation?

_____

Evaluation of Environment/Program

Room Schedule

TIME: **ACTIVITY:**

_____   _____

_____   _____

_____   _____

_____   _____

_____   _____

_____   _____

_____   _____

_____   _____

_____   _____

_____   _____

_____   _____

_____   _____

_____   _____

_____   _____

_____   _____

_____   _____

_____   _____

DAILY LESSON PLAN IS KEPT (LOCATION):

_____

Sample Medical Information

ALLERGIES:

John Doe: Asthma; allergic to pollen, animals, and large quantities of milk

Sally Smith: Reaction to excessive strawberries, jelly

PHYSICAL LIMITATIONS:

Bill Brown   Orthopedic problems; must sit on bottom, not on knees

Mary Jones   Orthopedic problems; special shoes for play, corrective shoes for sleeping; sit in chair, not on knees

NOTES OR OTHER SPECIAL INSTRUCTIONS:

Building on the Research

6

Medical Research Support for Child Care Practices

In the past few years, we have been inundated with medical research on early brain development. This research offers the child care field a solid foundation on which to build its practices. What we are learning does not change the traditional fundamentals of quality child care. It validates them. The newest research shows just how critical love, attention, play, and security are to the development of healthy, happy, well-adjusted adults. The experiences of the early years lay down the foundation on which all later learning will be built. It is our job to make these years count.

The 1990s was coined "The Decade of the Brain," and Rob Reiner began the "I Am Your Child Campaign." The Carnegie Foundation funded the *Starting Points* collaboration, which organized the research and pointed out the clear applications. From the Carnegie project emerged five key findings of the neuroscience research that provide a framework for us to use in application and in communication.

Key Findings and Implications of the Research

Let's look at the key findings and their implications for quality child care programs.

Finding 1: Brain development is contingent on a complex interplay between genes and environment.

Implications for Child Care: Environment

Things to think about:
- Rest and Nutrition—Proper rest and nutrition affect the alertness and the development of the brain.
- Safety—Children cannot learn when they do not feel safe.
- Toys and Equipment—Toys and equipment need to be colorful, multi-sensory, and challenging.
- Space—Children need space in order to enhance motor development.

Subjects & Predicates

- Colors—Some colors make us more alert while other colors calm us.
- Plants—Plants increase the oxygen in the environment—the brain needs sufficient oxygen.
- Aromas—Just like colors, some aromas increase alertness while others calm us.
- Water—Thirsty brains can't think.
- Adequate Stimulation—Children need some visual stimulation, but too much visual stimulation will interfere with children's ability to process information.

Finding 2: Early experiences contribute to brain structure and capacities.

Implications for Child Care: Curriculum

Things to think about:
- Focus and Reflection—Children need to be focused before instruction begins and they need time to reflect on what they have learned.
- Multi-sensory—The more senses involved in the learning situation, the more likely the child is to process the information.

Subjects & Predicates

- Interests of the Children—When children are interested, they are more likely to focus on the information and process the information.
- Provides Repetition—Repetition strengthens brain connections.
- Patterns—Intelligence is in large part our ability to see patterns and build relationships on those patterns.
- Music and Movement—Music provides release from anxiety, an emotional boost, repetition, and patterns. Movement enhances motor development.
- Assessment—Assessment allows the caregiver to know where children are developmentally and to prepare instruction accordingly.

Finding 3: Early interactions affect brain "wiring."

Implications for Child Care: Staffing

Things to think about:
- Hiring—Children need interactions with warm, loving adults. Finding the right person for the job should be a high priority when hiring staff.
- Retaining—Children need to develop relationships with their primary caregiver. It is disruptive to this process when staff come and go. Every effort should be made to hire people who are likely to stay committed to the job and to make retention of staff a high priority.

Subjects & Predicates

Finding 4: Brain development is non-linear.

Implications for Child Care: Staff Training

Things to think about:

- New Employee Training—Employees who are properly trained are far more likely to be effective in the classroom.
- Staff Training—Staff members need to be trained to know what windows of opportunity are and how they can use what they know about them to create classroom activities that take advantage of the windows (see chart on the following page).
- Release Time for Training—Finding ways to give employees relief time for training encourages them to obtain training.

Nancy Alexander

- Continuous Training—Training can take many forms. Place an article on the latest research in the staff lounge for reading. Think of ways to extend training.
- Follow up Training—Provide follow up for training. Everyone learns better when they can apply and evaluate what they learn.
- Recognition for Training—Finding ways to recognize staff members who attend training sessions increases their willingness to participate in training.

Windows of Opportunity

Window for:	Wiring Window	Greatest Enhancement Opportunity	Further Enhancement Possible
Emotional Intelligence	0-48 months	4-8 years	At any age
Motor Development	0-24 months	2-5 years	Decreases with age
Vision	0-24 months	2-6 years	
Early Sounds	4-8 months	8 mos.-10 years	
Music	0-36 months	3-10 years	
Thinking Skills	0-48 months	4-12 years	At any age
Reading Skills	0-24 months	2-7 years	At any age
Sound Language	0-60 months	6-10 years	Decreases with age

Finding 5: A child's brain is 2½ times as active as an adult's.

Implications for Child Care: Communication

Things to think about:

- Newsletters—Add information about brain development in your newsletters.
- Parent Seminars—Hold seminars for parents to help them understand the latest research.
- Newspaper/Magazine Articles—Write articles on the research for local newspapers and magazines.
- Brochures—Develop brochures on early brain development for dissemination to the families in your center and to the community at large.
- Speaking to Groups—Prepare short speeches on the subject of early brain development and deliver them to groups (Rotary, PTO, and so on) in your area.
- Notes Home to Families—Include tidbits about the research in your notes home to families.
- Public Policy Awareness—Stay abreast of what is going on in legislation. Communicate your ideas to legislators about bills based on brain and/or early childhood education research.

The previous list is only a place to begin. The implications of the research on early brain development for child care are practically endless. For the first time in a long time, attention is on the early years. We have hard science, with hard data, on which to base and support our practices.

The early brain development research offers an opportunity to take a major step forward in developing quality child care programs. As the research from the neuroscience community continues to unfold, you need to be ready to translate it into appropriate practices for your center. It is your role as director. It is your part of the partnership that is developing between science and education.

Recommended Reading

Armstrong, T. (2000). *Multiple intelligences in the classroom* (2nd ed.). Alexandria, VA: ASCD.

Begley, S. (1997). How to build a baby's brain. *Newsweek*. Special Edition, (Spring/Summer), 28-32.

Carnegie Corporation of New York (1994). *Starting points: Meeting the needs of our youngest children*. New York, NY: Carnegie Corporation.

Dennison, P. & G. Dennison. (1994). *Brain gym* (teacher's revised ed.). Ventura, CA: Edu Kinesthetics.

Hancock, L. & P. Wingart. (1997). The new preschool. *Newsweek*. Special Edition, (Spring/Summer), 36-37.

Healy, J.M. (1987). *Your child's growing mind: A guide to learning and brain development from birth to adolescence*. New York: Doubleday.

Houston, J. (1982). *The possible human: A course in enhancing your physical, mental, and creative abilities*. Los Angeles, CA: Jeremy Tarcher.

Jensen, E. (1998). *Teaching with the brain in mind*. Alexandria, VA: ASCD.

Jensen, E. (2000). *Brain-based learning*. San Diego, CA: Brain Store, Inc.

Nash, M. (1997). Fertile minds. *Time*, 148(5, February 3), 48-56.

Ramey, C.T. & S.L. Ramey. (1999). *Right from birth*. NY: Goddard Press.

Schiller, P. (1999) *Start smart: Building brain power in the early years*. Beltsville, MD: Gryphon House.

Schiller, P. (1999). Turning knowledge into practice. *Child Care Information Exchange*. (March/April).

Schiller, P. (1999). The thinking brain. *Child Care Information Exchange*. (May/June) (order #12149).

Schiller, P. (1997). Brain development research: Support and challenges. *Child Care Information Exchange*. (September/October).

Shore, R. (1996). *Rethinking the brain: New insights into early development*. Chicago, IL: Families and Work Institute.

Sousa, D.A. (2000). *How the brain learns: A classroom teacher's guide* (2nd ed.). Thousand Oaks, CA: Corwin Press.

Sylwester, R. (1995) *A Celebration of neurons: An educator's guide to the human brain*. Alexandria, VA: ASCD.

Your child: From birth to three. (2000). *Newsweek*. Special Edition, (Fall/Winter).

Internet Resources

I Am Your Child Campaign
335 North Maple Drive, Suite 135
Beverly Hills, CA 90210
(310) 285-2385
Web: http://www.iamyourchild.org

Zero to Three: National Center for Infants, Toddlers, and Families
734 15th Street, NW, Tenth Floor
Washington, DC 20005-2101
(202) 638-1144 or (800) 899-4301 for Publications
Web: http://www.zerotothree.org

National Association for the Education of Young Children (NAEYC)
1834 Connecticut Avenue, NW
Washington, DC 20009-6786
(800) 424-2460
Web: http://www.naeyc.org

National Childcare Information Center
Web: http://www.nccic.org

insights

ST. LUKE'S DAY SCHOOL

St. Luke's United Methodist Church   November, No. 2

calendar

vember 5—Chapel
 classes—9:15 a.m.
rents welcome

vember 5—Rotunda
rent Meeting—7:30 p.m.

vember 6 & 7
eech/Hearing Testing

vember 12-16
rent/Teacher Conferences

vember 22 & 23
ANKSGIVING HOLIDAY

vember 30
yground Committee—
30 a.m.

From Pat Dyke, Day School Director

...But in truth I understand nothing about it except this, that the greatest and most important difficulty in human knowledge seems to lie in the branch of knowledge which deals with the upbringing and education of children...The manifestations of their inclinations is so slight and so obscure at that early age, the promise so uncertain and so misleading, that it is hard to lease any solid judgment on them.
—Montaigne, 1588

We view family-teacher conferences as a sharing time, with both "school" and "home" providing insights as to the nature of the child, then planning together to meet the child's needs as we both see them.

Your child's teacher has been making notes on a progress chart that addresses all areas of development: social, emotional, physical, and intellectual. The teacher has observed the child as he or she interacts with others, uses equipment and media, participates in the motor and music programs, and shows enthusiasm about the environment.

We do not see our role at this time as making predictions about your child's future, but rather as *describing* the child at school, learning more about him or her from you, and taking positive steps in programming activities that will enable optimal growth.

One of my greatest pleasures as director of this school is in coming to know you, who care so much about your children and their education.

Where Is Your Child Going After St. Luke's?

I am increasingly aware of the challenges you face in ensuring that your children are given the opportunity for quality education. As noted in the quote from Montaigne, this is not a new concern. (You might enjoy reading his essay, "Of the Education of Children.")

I do feel, however, that as parents, we must take a look at this problem from all angles. For example, how does the tension of test taking, when so few are selected, affect the stress level of young children? What is the message to the young mind, which cannot process information about what is going on in the same way that an adult can? What can we do as a society of caring people in Houston to change this situation of too few places for the numbers of eligible children?

We do not suggest that we have the answers to a family's questions, but only to offer to help wherever we can. Children—all children—deserve a quality education; they also must have their time in the sun!

Parent Meeting

We hope that our Parent Meeting on November 5th will be informative and provocative. It will be fast-paced and address issues that you have asked to hear about: How Young Children Learn, Safety, and the Suzuki Method of Music (Talent) Education. We hope to see you in the Rotunda at 7:30 p.m.

Parent Volunteer News

A big thanks to everyone who helped make the brightly colored smocks for our teachers. You handled the difficulty of cutting out the pieces with *no extra* fabric very calmly!

We need help with the *resource closet* and the *library*. Any morning or afternoon that you can give us some time, we would appreciate it.

When you come in to help, will you please sign in at the office? We'd like to keep a record of your service to the school.

Nutrition

Snacks: If you would like to send in a nutritious snack for your child's class, feel free to do so. We have been asked about this, and the staff feels that it would be an opportunity for greater variation in snacks and for parents and children to have fun preparing the food together.

Ideas for snacks are:

Stuffed celery	Fresh fruit
Carrot sticks	Fresh vegetables
Yogurt	Frozen fruit bars
	Cheesecakes

On the advice of a family physician, we do not serve nuts to the children. *Please let the teacher know* if you plan to send in a snack for the class.

Safety

The clothing that children wear to school needs to be suitable for play. Just imagine trying to use playground equipment in a frilly dress, with bare legs and slippery shoes. We admit that the children look adorable in their beautiful clothes, but we ask for your help in making sure they are dressed to benefit fully from the school program.

Questions to ask yourself when dressing your child for day school:

Are closings easy to manipulate?

Can pants be taken down and up again with relative ease?

Is the child wearing sneakers to prevent slipping?

"Thank you so much for your help with this problem!"
            –from all the teachers.

From the Day School Office

Toddler 2s

The two-year-old classes had a special treat this month when one of our parents, Peggy Hill, presented a puppet show, "Kermit and Friends." Thank you, Peggy!

During October, the 2s learned about colors, shapes, and sizes, and, of course, we celebrated Halloween. We carved jack-o'-lanterns and wore costumes to school.

Mrs. Lowry, our motor teacher, is now giving two-year-olds a lesson once a month. The children will be dancing with scarves, batting balloons, moving their bodies through obstacle courses, and doing other activities that help develop their large muscles.

Thursday-Friday 2s

Rhymes and Reason. The two-year-olds were on the playground, and several boys were climbing the ladder to the fort. One little fellow was having great difficulty getting down in a prescribed safe manner. After a lot of explaining and just short of a rescue, the teacher asked him, "Where are your feet?" From inside the fort came an echo, "Where's the beef?" followed by a second echo, "Where's Mrs. O'Keef?" The last was a reference to our beloved music teacher, Mrs. Paula O'Keef. It must have done the trick, because the stranded climber returned safely to the ground.

—*L. Smythe*

Pre-nursery

From the Terrific 3s

The 3s have really been busy since our last newsletter! Not only are they reinforcing facts and skills that they already know, but they are also learning new things all the time! Our weekly topics have emphasized shapes,

colors, and sizes, and one week, we learned about pets. This included an exciting trip to an animal hospital (where we saw how our pet friends receive special care) and a classroom visit from Fred, Mat Parker's floppy-eared rabbit.

Two other exciting events the 3s experienced were a puppet show by one of the school's parents and picture taking. (The children loved being in the "spotlight!")

In the classroom, the 3s continue to experiment with clay, glue, paint, crayons, and scissors. They are also increasing their perceptual and motor skills through games, puzzles, finger plays, and much more. Socially, they are learning to communicate their feelings and are enjoying more cooperative play—they are very imaginative in these areas!

And finally, the 3s have been learning safety rules, which were especially stressed during Halloween. We are thankful that everyone had a safe and fun-filled night of trick-or-treating.

Parents: Your three-year-olds really enjoy your participation in the classroom. If you would like to help with a special art project or bring in a special snack, please let your child's teacher know. Snacks from home are really great! (Remember to check with the teacher about allergies.)

Special note: Jennifer Myers and Sarah Jones have both become "big sisters" since the last newsletter. Both of them are in Mrs. Smith's class and they were both surprised with baby brothers. Congratulations to them and their parents!

Nursery Department

In October our three-day class of four-year-olds went on an exciting field trip to the Guest Quarters Hotel, with Robin Massey's Dad as our host. We toured the kitchen and laundry, and had juice and cupcakes in a suite on the fifteenth floor.

Justin Jacobs' dad came in during October when we were studying jobs, and talked to us about the construction business. He showed us slides, and we worked with hammers and nails after his visit.

Captain Charles Bragg from the Harris County Sheriff's office visited the 4s on October 15. Thank you, Captain Charles!

—*M. Dawson*

Kindergarten Department

Bridge Class

The Bridge Class really enjoyed Halloween! We loved the piñata from our party moms, Ruby Day, Nita Page, and Patty Smith. All kinds of strange visitors appeared at our party, including Dorothy and Toto, several Simbas, a Grinch, a moon-jumper, and a three-headed spaceman. A celebrity from Blues Clues, a prima ballerina, Casper, and Woodstock also attended. Of course, the presence of a couple of vampires and a wicked witch made our Halloween party complete!

Before Halloween, we discussed "real" and "pretend" at circle time. This provided a balance to the violent nature of the characters and costumes chosen by the children.

We're looking forward to practicing our culinary skills by making a traditional Thanksgiving feast. It should be an exciting month as we learn about the first Americans and the early settlers.
Our October birthdays were Benjamin Kirth and Travis Allen. Congratulations!!!

—*P. Miralow & N. Denison*

Kindergarten

We've been working with the magic of vowels (A, E, I, O, and U), beginning sounds, middle sounds, and rhyming words. We're so proud of our fully illustrated book—please stop by and see it. In science and math, we're enjoying one-more, one-less, and equal games; numbers; and the numerals 1-20. Our Spanish, music, yoga, and nature activities are well underway, as well as our playground, caroling, and dance activities.

—*A. Benson*

A Final Note from Pat Dyke

Please be sure to bring in a tote bag for each child in Extended Day. Also, kindly refrain from having children bring toys to Extended Day because these items get lost and there is not enough space to store all of them.

Your cooperation is appreciated. Thank you!

Small Talk

April, 2000

This month's issue of Small Talk is dedicated to building self-esteem.

Building Self-Esteem

Self-esteem is fundamentally important to behavior and happiness. If children believe that they are what they should be, then their self-esteem is high. However, if they think that they are less than they should be, then their self-esteem is low. For children to develop positive self-esteem, they must acquire a realistic belief that they are competent human beings and they must have a feeling of worthiness.

Although self-esteem develops from the inside and from a child's own perceptions, it is influenced by outside experiences and perceptions. The majority of those outside influences come from families.

Your attitude toward your children is of prime importance. Children are extremely sensitive to your tone of voice, your speed of talking, your posture, your mouth and eyes, and your touch. They watch you for signs of acceptance.

It is important to give your children lots of opportunities for success. In part, this is dependent on having appropriate expectations. When children are expected to make a bed before they are capable, or to read before they are ready, they develop a sense of failure. All children develop at individual paces, and staying in tune with that development is key to children developing healthy self-esteem.

The newest research indicates that self-esteem and problem solving are linked together. When children are allowed to solve child-size problems, they grow in self-confidence. Children can often think of solutions to their squabbles with a friend over a favorite toy or solutions to getting their ball out from under a chair. Think about how you feel when you solve a problem. Then remember how good that feeling is before jumping in and solving your children's problems for them.

Providing for success is important, but it must be balanced with some challenges. If we never let children fail, they develop an unrealistic sense of self that will someday backfire. Children need to learn that some successes only come over time and with work. It is these accomplishments that really solidify our self-esteem.

Self-esteem develops over time. Every experience contributes to the overall picture. Make the most of the journey and before you know it, your child will be a well-adjusted, healthy young adult.

Things You Can Do:

- Recognize your child's successes. Can she tie her shoes? Can he blow a bubble? Has she learned to drink from a straw? Has he learned to clap?

- Respect your child's uniqueness. Is she good at paying attention to details? Is he especially kind to others?

- Encourage your child to solve his or her own problems when possible.

  Ask your child:

     How can you take a third toy when your hands are full with the two you already have?

     How can you get your kite out of the tree?

     There are three children and only two trucks. How can all three play?

  Discuss the steps you take when solving a problem.

- Allow your child the freedom to explore and take risks.

  Stay close by when she is climbing, but don't hover.

  Let him play at a friend's house for a while on Saturday.

  Allow her to spend the night outdoors in her fort (under a watchful eye).

- Make sure your child feels like he or she is playing a contributing role in the family.

  Talk to him about decisions that you are making. Listen to his opinion.

  Give her jobs to do that are within her ability, such as making her bed, setting the table, drying the dishes, and helping prepare dinner.

- Let your child share in decision making.

  Encourage her to make a suggestion about which color of car she likes best. Take her

suggestion seriously even if you decide on another color.

Share verbally the steps you take when you are making a decision.

- Show your child that you value and love her or him unconditionally when she or he behaves and when he or she misbehaves.

  Help him see that punishment is the logical consequence of a poor choice he has made.

  Let her know that we all make poor choices sometimes.

  Apologize when you are wrong.

  Always discuss why the child's behavior was unacceptable.

Library Corner (books related to self-esteem)

A Chair for My Mother by Vera Williams
Amazing Grace by Mary Hoffman
Bravo, Tanya! by Satomi Ichikawa
Dance, Tanya by Satomi Ichikawa
Peter's Chair by Ezra Jack Keats
Whistle for Willie by Ezra Jack Keats

Resources for Families

Brazelton, T.B. & S.I. Greenspan. (2000). *The irreducible needs of children: What every child must have to grow, learn, and flourish.* Cambridge, MA: Perseus Books.

Goleman, D. (1997). *Emotional intelligence.* New York: Bantam Books.

Ramey, C.T. & S.L. Ramey. (1999). *Right from birth.* New York: Goddard Press.

Notes from School

*Remember that each child needs to bring two hard-boiled eggs to school for the egg dying on Friday.
*Registrations for next year are due by April 30th.
*Ms. Katie's birthday is April 28th.

Newsletter Resources

Pages, Inc.
P.O. Box 6036
Colorado Springs, CO 80934
719-632-0916

Pages, Inc publishes Parent Pages, which is a preprinted newsletter that can be purchased for a modest fee. It can be customized for your center by adding your name and logo. One page can be left blank for you to add specific information related to your center.

Dear _____,

It has come to my attention that your child's tuition has not been paid for the week of _____. It is center policy that all tuitions are paid in advance of the week of care. Teachers are scheduled and menus are prepared based on enrollment.

Your prompt attention to this matter is greatly appreciated.

Sincerely,

Sample #1
Tuition Collection

Dear _____,

Your child's tuition continues to be past due. As you are aware, all tuitions are due in advance of care.

Our records indicate that you owe $_____ for the week/s of _____.

If tuition is not paid by tomorrow morning, we will not be able to accept (child's name) into care.

Sincerely,

Sample #2 More Than One Week
Past Due Tuition Collection

Sample #3 New Infant Enrollee Welcome

Dear _____,

Since the health and safety of your baby is a vital concern to us both, we would like to tell you about our sleep and rest procedures.

We change the crib sheets each morning and as often as needed during the day.

We are careful about what toys we allow in the crib. We do not string toys across the crib.

We place infants on their backs for sleep.

We record the time and length of each nap on a daily chart.

Infants vary in their need for sleep, so rest time is individualized as much as possible.

We encourage you to share information about your baby with us as we work together to provide a secure and happy environment for your little one.

Sincerely,

Dear Families,

During our morning check of the children, we discovered a child with head lice. The child was sent home. This is not an uncommon event in group care situations. However, in order to keep the lice from spreading, we will all need to work together.

To avoid infestation, it is important to inspect all family members for at least two weeks and treat if infected. Nits on the scalp may be seen most easily on the hair at the back of the neck and above the ears.

If a family member is infested, you will need to sterilize all of his or her personal clothing, sheets, and blankets by washing them in water that is at least 130°F. Dry cleaning also works. Be sure to disinfect combs and brushes, too. There are effective shampoos and creams for the treatment of lice. Please consult your doctor.

Please be assured that the child care center is doing everything possible to prevent infestation. With your support, we will stop the lice from spreading.

Please feel free to call us with any questions.

Sincerely,

For extensive information on head lice check
http://www.headlice.org/publications/ccguide.html

Sample #5 Health Tips

Dear Family,

Healthy children are happier children, and healthier children are better prepared to succeed in school.

What children eat, how they play, and the amount of sleep they get, together with expressions of love, support, and caring, are the basis for their health.

Health Tips:

Eating Habits: The natural, traditional food of any culture is basically healthful. In contrast, highly processed food is usually unhealthy because it is poor in nutrients and rich in sugar and preservatives. If you train your children to enjoy fruits and vegetables instead of candy and packaged desserts, and to prefer natural fruit juice and water to soft drinks, you will be developing healthier eating habits in your children.

Sleep: Children need a great deal of sleep to be able to be healthy and to remain alert and attentive during the day. The younger the child, the more sleep he or she needs. Up to the age of eight, children generally do best when they get ten hours of sleep each day.

Play: Play is essential to children's growth. During play, children exercise their bodies and their imaginations. They learn to understand the world around them. Play can be quiet and solitary or active and involve others. Children need time to play. They need space to run, jump, climb, and slide, either alone or with others.

Watching television interferes with play. It is a passive and unchallenging activity. Television is also filled with violence and information that is too sophisticated for young minds. You will be doing your children a great favor by limiting their television viewing. When they do watch, help them select programs that are educational.

Encourage children to run and play, cut and paste, draw and paint, construct with blocks and boxes, play musical instruments and sing. Encourage them to use their imaginations. Stay away from mechanical toys that do everything automatically.

Have fun with your children. Healthy food, rest, and play are good for you, too.

Sincerely,

Sample #6
Spending Quality Time with Children

Dear Family,

Working and balancing home life is a difficult task. You probably find yourself wondering if you are making the most of the limited time you have with your child. Quality far surpasses quantity when it comes to little ones. Here are some suggestions for making the most of your available hours with your children.

- Make mornings relaxed. Encourage children to choose their clothes for the next day the night before. Get up early enough to give yourself some time before waking the rest of the family so you will feel satisfied and unhurried. Keep breakfast simple.

- Make use of the daily travel time to the center. Establish meaningful routines such as asking the children to choose the radio station in the morning while you choose in the evening. Note the time on the bank clock. Keep a pillow in the car for a little more snoozing or cuddling. Talk about what you and your children are going to do that day.

- Make a smooth transition from car to classroom by walking into the center with your child. Talk to the teacher, give your child a hug, tell her you love her, say goodbye, and remind her you will be back at the end of the day.

- Create lunchtime events. Occasionally show up and have lunch with your child or bring a sack lunch and take your child to the park.

- Investigate flextime with your employer. It may be possible to work overtime or through a lunch hour so you can have time off to help with the Christmas party or attend a particular program.

- When you pick up your child from the center, make going home an adventure. Encourage him to talk about his day. Share your work experiences. Sing songs. Have an occasional surprise in the car, such as a folded fan made from office stationary or an empty plastic staple box.

- Schedule dinner for success. Perhaps you may want to allow your child to have a nutritious snack when you get home to tide her over until you can get dinner prepared. Encourage her to help you set the table.

- Establish firm bedtime routines. After bath, it's time for a story and then bed. Spending ten minutes here with your little one snuggled against you is more beneficial that an hour of dragged out interruptions. After a hug and a kiss, the rest of the evening is yours.

• Share your days off with your child. Use a portion of the day for yourself and save a portion to spend doing something both you and your child will enjoy.

Spending quality time with your child will create a lasting impression for both of you. You will have memories to last a lifetime.

Sincerely,

Dear Family,

Discipline means teaching children the rules that people live by and directing them so they will adopt these rules on their own accord. Your goal should be to guide toward self-discipline.

Discipline and punishment are not the same. The purpose of punishment is to prevent children from repeating a forbidden act. Usually, punishment is a short-term deterrent and is only effective if it can be enforced. In contrast, the purpose of discipline is to direct children in choosing constructive behavior patterns and in developing self-control and self-discipline.

Here are some suggestions for things you can do to help guide your child toward self-discipline.

- Make suggestions in a positive way. "Bounce the ball on the floor" is a positive suggestion. It tells your child what to do. "Don't hit the window" is a negative suggestion. It only tells the child what not to do. Telling children what they should do is far more effective than constant reminders of what not to do. The words "stop" and "don't" are used so frequently with children that they lose their effect. Try to save these words for occasions when you must put a quick stop to the child's behavior for safety's sake (for example, if the child is getting ready to touch a hot stove).

- Use your tone of voice to convey messages. The child eventually blocks out shouting, which requires the adult to get louder and louder to get attention. Instead of shouting, try using a calm but firm voice.

- Set limits. Children learn impulse control between the ages of two and four. This is the fertile time when they are most receptive to developing the understanding that they cannot act on impulse. You should set limits to protect children's health and safety, protect the rights of others, and protect children from their own strong feelings. However, setting limits must be balanced with providing opportunities for children to explore and develop. Too many limits are restrictive and will only make children resentful and anxious to reach the day when they will no longer be under your control.

- Choose words that build confidence. Labeling children as bad or naughty may cause them to lose confidence in themselves. It is better to show disapproval of what children are doing than to show disapproval of children themselves. Saying, "Tiffany, keep your food on your plate" helps Tiffany more than, "You are a bad girl to make all that work for your mother." Telling children, "Daddy won't love you" threatens them with loss of love, which is more than they can bear. Contrary to the way it seems, children prefer to do what their parents expect of them, and they behave better when they sense that they are loved. When you are guiding children, if you can say, "I don't like what you did but I still like you," you're on the right track.

- Keep your suggestions and directions to a minimum. Offering too many suggestions to children can prevent them from solving their own problems and using their own ideas. Children need a chance to work out their own problems. When you do give directions, expect them to be followed. You may have to back up your words with actions. If telling Steve to go to bed brings no response, smile at him, gently take his hand, and lead him to the bedroom.

- Most of all, have fun together. Families who play together, work together, and share their interests and experiences develop relationships based on mutual respect, love, affection, and feelings of belonging. This kind of closeness leads to cooperation.

(Name of Center) is sponsoring a Positive Guidance Seminar on Tuesday, May 25th, from 6:30 to 8:00 p.m. Babysitting will be available. If you are interested, please sign up with your child's teacher.

Sincerely,

These employment packets have been designed for the classroom teacher and the teacher's assistant or aide. Go through these features and adapt them to your particular requirements and policies.

Teachers and Head Teachers

Contents of Professional Employment Packet
- Organizational Chart
- Professional Standards
- Personal Recognition
- Employer Policies
- Responsibilities of the Professional Employee
- Position Descriptions
- Conditions for Employment: Staff
- Summary of Benefits
- Termination
- Grievance Procedures
- Statement of Principles

Professional Standards

Professionals are individuals who, with adequate training, experience, intellectual capacity, and moral integrity, effectively devote their skills and knowledge to the service of society and their profession in whatever assignment they find themselves. They are fully aware of the personal responsibility and trusteeship conferred by their special training.

Regardless of educational background, no individual can expect to be regarded as truly professional unless he or she adopts a code of conduct and an attitude that reflect a desire to contribute to society and to the profession. Obviously, if a professional person forfeits this code of conduct and attitude, and the freedom to act in accordance with them, whether that forfeiture is to the employer or anyone else, that individual has destroyed the foundation upon which professional status was erected.

Personal Recognition

This center recognizes its obligation to encourage professional attitudes among its staff. We have an obligation to teach others and to uphold the reputation of the profession. Consideration of the employer's attitude toward the professional teacher has led to a number of tested principles, which are applicable to all staff:

- Recognizing each person as an individual and always providing an opportunity for expression of his or her own views.
- Encouraging advancement and stimulating professional interest by adopting methods by which progress can be measured.
- Instituting an ongoing training program.
- Making certain that each person is informed periodically of his or her progress and needs.
- Helping each person learn to appreciate the qualities of leadership and to develop his or her own leadership talents.

Employer Policies

1. The employer should keep professional employees informed of the organization's objectives, policies, and programs.
2. The employer should provide the professional employee with compensation (salary and other benefits) commensurate with the professional's contribution, taking into account the employee's abilities, professional status, responsibilities, education, and experience, and the potential value of the work to be performed.
3. Each position should be properly classified as to its level in the overall salary structure. The evaluation of each position should include such factors as the problem-solving skills required and the accountability for an action and its consequences.
4. Duties, levels of responsibility, and the relationship of positions within the organizational hierarchy should be clearly defined and accurately reflected in position titles.
5. The employer should conduct a performance review with each professional employee at appropriate intervals (at least once a year). The review should cover how well the employee has performed his or her work, areas for improvement, and discussion of career planning, including the viewpoints of both the employer and the employee. The professional employee should be informed if his or her performance is

unsatisfactory. The employer should document the results of the review.
6. The employer should provide office space, support staff, and physical facilities that promote the maximum personal efficiency of the professional employee.
7. The employer should not require the professional employee to accept responsibility for work not supervised or performed by that employee.

Responsibilities of the Professional Employee

1. The professional employee should maintain technical competence through a program of continuing education and broadening experience.
2. The professional employee should belong to and participate in the activities of appropriate organizations in order to obtain additional knowledge and experience.
3. The professional employee should achieve appropriate registration and/or certification as soon as he or she is eligible.
4. The early childhood professional is committed to the following principles:
   - To be accountable as an individual to the highest objective of the teaching profession, maintaining high standards of scholarship.
   - To be alert to the fact that his or her recommendations and actions may alter the lives of others.
   - To be aware of the need to refrain from undertaking any activity in which personal problems are likely to lead to inadequate performance.
   - To be aware of the rights of families and children in the area of confidentiality and in access to records.

Position Description

Teacher
A teacher is responsible to the center director for the implementation and ongoing success of the center's educational program. Teachers are expected to work and relate on a day-to-day basis with all age groups at the center.

Qualifications
1. Have a BA/BS degree in early childhood education or a related field, preferably. Have taken at least one course in early childhood education, and have at least one year experience as a preschool/child care teacher.
2. Be at least 18 years of age (or as required by law).
3. Be reliable and conscientious in carrying out assigned duties.
4. Demonstrate a patient and loving attitude toward young children.

5. Be flexible in working with children of different ages.
6. Be healthy and submit a recent health assessment from a medical doctor, including a T.B./P.D.D. shot.
7. Meet the requirements of law pertaining to convictions of felonies or misdemeanors.

Responsibilities

1. Plan and conduct daily activities for children in a safe environment.
2. Supervise personnel assigned to assist with daily group activities.
3. Prepare, outside of class time, educational materials needed to implement the daily activity plan.
4. Maintain a clean and orderly physical environment conducive to optimal growth and development of children, and use equipment and supplies conscientiously, signing them out and returning them to their proper place.
5. Attend and actively contribute to staff and family meetings.
6. Appropriately share information with other staff members, and serve as a resource person in a specific area.
7. Relate to families in order to better foster the growth and development of their children.

Head Teacher

The following qualifications were most frequently cited by *Child Care Information Exchange* participants as essential for a lead teacher (R. Neugebauer, 1978, Reprint #7 Staff Selection):

Disposition	Interaction with Children
Warmth	Nurturance
Sense of humor	Speech with children
Patience	Creativity
Openness	ECE philosophy
Confidence	Sensitive to individuals
	Ability to control

Competence	Interaction with Adults
Communication skills	Leadership
Organizing ability	Cooperation
Maturity	Peer relations

ECE knowledge   Parent relations
Intelligence and common sense

Work Behavior

Flexibility
Willingness to grow
Energy and enthusiasm
Dependability
Initiative
Commitment to children

Conditions for Employment: Staff

1. The employees of the center perform their jobs in accordance with the duties contained in the attached job description. All staff members are directly responsible to the director.

2. Full-time employees work 40 hours a week, and a part-time employee is one who works less than 40 hours a week. Increments in salary will be considered after six months of employment. The director is responsible for scheduling working hours with breaks to ensure adequate coverage.

3. Full-time, salaried employees will not receive compensation for overtime.

4. All members of the staff are asked to provide four weeks notice to the director prior to the effective date of resignation. A minimum of two weeks notice is mandatory.

5. Every staff member will be considered to be in probationary employment status during the first two months of employment. At the conclusion of the first two months of employment, there will be a formal review of the staff member's performance, and appropriate recommendations will be made to the staff member. At any time during the probationary period, resignation or dismissal may be accomplished with a minimum of one week's notice.

6. At the conclusion of every six months of employment, each employee will be evaluated.

7. Every employee shall provide a recent health assessment form upon entering the center and every 12 months thereafter.

8. Full-time and part-time employees will be paid on a monthly basis on the first Monday of every month.

Summary of Benefits

1. Medical/dental benefits plan
2. Life and accidental death insurance plans
3. Holidays—10 paid holidays (schedule to be posted)
4. Vacations—After three (3) months, full-time employees will accrue 15 days of paid vacation time each year. Vacations must be scheduled and approved in advance.
5. Sick days—Salaried employees will be allowed 15 days of paid sick leave per year. When absent for five or more consecutive days, the employee must provide a note from his or her physician. Employees should notify the director/administrator at the beginning of the day if they are unable to work that day.
6. Credit union—Offers savings and loan services at reasonable rates.
7. Jury duty—The center will make up the difference in pay when an employee is called for jury duty.
8. Death in the family—In the event of a death in an employee's immediate family, he or she will be allowed three days off with pay. Immediate family includes parents, grandparents, brothers, sisters, children, spouse, and spouse's parents.
9. Absences—Employees must call in when they are going to be absent. Failure to do so will be cause for termination.
10. Telephone use—A telephone is designated for staff use.

Termination

The employee or employer should give adequate notice of termination of employment, as appropriate.

Employee

1. If the employee decides to terminate employment, he or she should assist the employer in maintaining continuity of function, and should provide at least two weeks' notice.
2. Upon termination, the employee should maintain all proprietary information as confidential.

Employer

Dismissal shall be for cause. Dismissal procedures are as follows:

1. The center director shall give a verbal warning as the first notification to an employee of unsatisfactory performance.
2. As a second notification, the director shall give a written warning to an

employee, informing the person of specific areas needing improvement.

3. Finally, the director shall notify the staff member in writing that he or she is dismissed. In the letter, the director should specify the reasons and should review the steps taken previously.

It is the policy of the center to give every employee an opportunity to improve his or her work, attitude, or behavior.

A dismissed employee must be given two weeks' notice. However, immediate dismissal will result if the termination is due to flagrant abuse of trust or unacceptable behavior/conduct affecting the children.

Grievance Procedures

When a grievance situation arises, the person or persons involved should use the following procedure:

1. Bring the problem to the attention of the supervising teacher.
2. If not resolved, bring the problem to the director.
3. If a grievance is still not resolved, make an appointment with the board or person to whom the director reports.

A Statement of Principles of Early Childhood Education

It is the objective of the center to provide an environment and experiences that will foster the children's development to the highest potential.

The interactions of staff with children and their families should be compassionate and respectful. We strive to provide continuing and frequent opportunities for family involvement in the program.

We accept the responsibility to provide for the emotional needs of all children. Careful selection of staff as to their ability to respond to and understand children's needs for security is a priority. Once the child feels secure, the setting is designed to promote self-reliance, cooperation, and consideration of others.

The program is comprehensive in scope, accepts each child at his or her stage of development, and provides for all aspects of development: social, emotional, physical, and intellectual.

Areas of concern in our center include:

- Nonsexist approach to the realization of the children's potential
- Identification of children with special problems
- Programming to meet the needs of each child
- Nurturing of children's self-esteem, initiative, concern for others, and creative thinking
- The role of older children in the development of younger ones
- The role of senior citizens in the development of the young

The following declaration was adopted by the United Nations on November 20, 1959. It sums up very well how the center feels about the rights of the children we serve:

1. The right to equality, regardless of race, color, sex, religion, nationality, or social origin.
2. The right to develop physically and mentally in a healthy manner.
3. The right to a name and nationality.
4. The right to adequate nutrition, housing and medical services.
5. The right to special care, if handicapped.
6. The right to love, understanding and protection.
7. The right to free education, to play and recreation.
8. The right to be among the first to receive relief in times of disaster.
9. The right to protection against all forms of neglect, cruelty and exploitation.
10. The right to be brought up in a spirit of tolerance, peace and universal brotherhood.

Teachers' Aides

Contents of Employment Packet
- Organizational Chart*
- Position Description
- Conditions for Employment*
- Summary of Benefits*
- Termination*
- Grievance Procedures*
- Statement of Principles*

*As in Professional Employment Packet

Position Description

Along with the teacher, the teacher's aide cares for the children and works to build an environment within the school that provides the children with positive and enriching experiences. The teacher's aide serves as assistant to the teacher, under the supervision of the center's director.

Qualifications

1. Be at least 18 years of age (or as required by law).
2. Have some experience working with young children.
3. Be reliable and conscientious in carrying out assigned duties.
4. Demonstrate a patient and loving attitude toward young children.
5. Be flexible in working with different age groups.
6. Be healthy and submit a recent health assessment from a physician, including a T.B./P.D.D. shot (as required by law).
7. Have completed courses in early childhood education (beneficial but not mandatory).
8. Must not have been convicted of any offenses as stated in regulations, as required by law.

Duties

1. Interact with children in a manner that clearly conveys love and acceptance.
2. Respond to children by touching, holding, smiling, and speaking in a positive tone of voice.
3. Assist children in developing self-help skills.
4. Initiate classroom activities and cooperate with child-initiated activities and explorations.
5. Participate in supervising free play and outdoor play.
6. Supervise and assist children with clean up.
7. Assist and supervise children during toileting period.
8. Help teachers with weekly lesson planning.
9. Assist teachers with children's individual assessment forms.
10. Keep anecdotal records, under the supervision of the teacher.
11. Attend and participate in staff meetings and in-service training sessions.
12. Participate in family-teacher conferences at teacher's discretion.

Job Descriptions of Support Staff

Food Service Supervisor

The food service supervisor reports to the center director. The goal of the food service supervisor is to provide nutritionally balanced snacks and meals for all children enrolled. Children learn to eat foods that contribute to good health as they participate in a snack or meal program that introduces them to a wide variety of tastes, textures, and temperatures, and a sampling of a wide range of nutritious foods (for example, raw vegetables, cheese and cottage cheese, fruit drinks, and so on). Their enjoyment and enthusiasm are enhanced if the children help prepare and serve their own food, and if the foods they eat at mealtimes are used to promote social interaction, vocabulary building, and other educational goals.

Qualifications

1. Must have experience in quality cooking.
2. Must be healthy and submit a yearly health assessment from a medical doctor (including a negative T.B./Mantoux test).
3. Must attend a workshop every year pertaining to nutrition and food preparation.
4. Must be reliable and conscientious in carrying out duties.
5. Must be able to relate well to children.
6. Must have an understanding of the nutritional needs of children in order to work with the dietician.

Duties

The following responsibilities are to be carried out in accordance with the guidelines established by the dietician:

1. Requisition appropriate amounts of food at established intervals and prepare designated menus.
2. Store food appropriately, both before and after cooking, in bins, cupboards, or refrigerators.
3. Prepare vegetables by washing, scraping, peeling, chopping, and so on.
4. Cook vegetables, meats, sauces, desserts, and so on.
5. Record amounts of food, including milk, used daily.
6. Wash and sterilize dishes, pots, and utensils after meals.
7. Clean refrigerator, stove, bins, and cupboards according to a designated schedule.
8. Scrub counters and sinks after meals.
9. Wash dishtowels after use.
10. Sweep and mop kitchen floor.

11. Assume duties as requested by director.
12. Assign duties and supervise food service assistants.
13. Constantly monitor procedures to follow safety standards for the staff and children.

Food Service Assistant(s)

The food service assistant is responsible to the food service supervisor for designated daily duties as assigned, including those listed above.

Assistant/Receptionist

The assistant/receptionist reports directly to the center director.

Qualifications
1. Typing skills
2. Spelling skills
3. Grammatical skills
4. Telephone manners

Duties
1. Handle all calls and visitors with courtesy and tact.
2. Other duties as designated by the center director.

Custodian

The custodian is responsible for the general maintenance of the building and grounds, and will keep them in a hygienic, safe, and presentable condition. The custodian will arrange for outside services as they become necessary to keep the building and grounds in repair. The custodian reports directly to the center director.

Qualifications
1. Experience in the care and maintenance of buildings and grounds.
2. Basic knowledge of common household repairs and simple gardening techniques.
3. Willingness to participate in some in-service training in child development.
4. Ability to relate well to children.

Duties

1. Maintain floors and keep walls, doors, furnishings, and fixtures clean, safe, operable, and presentable.
2. Sanitize toilets and washbasins daily, making sure to adequately supply toilet tissue, paper towels, and soap dispensers.
3. Keep entrances, walks, steps, and so on swept and free of debris and other obstructions.
4. Maintain electrical fixtures, performing minor repairs as needed.
5. Change light bulbs.
6. Keep garden and grounds neat and attractive at all times. Children will be asked to assist in gardening and other chores and, on occasion, with some indoor chores as well.
7. Help keep the kitchen in a safe, sanitary condition.
8. Assist in setting up and putting away heavy equipment.
9. Miscellaneous other tasks as designated by the center director.

Give the development of your Faculty Manual careful consideration. Think through your personal values and your philosophy on early childhood education and state them in clear terms. If you are precise about your ideas on how children should be nurtured and what you consider suitable program content and implementation, your staff will be better able to meet your expectations.

Each person working in your center, regardless of position, should receive a copy of the manual. This gives the food service supervisor, for instance, an understanding of the philosophy of the center and specific ideas as to how you want adults to interact with the children. It also gives the teachers' aides a mini-course in child care. We have found that a carefully prepared manual sets a tone for staff and makes a clear statement about the professionalism of the administration. You can use the sample manual included in this appendix as a model. Of course, you should adapt it to the specific policies and procedures of your center. Explanations and comments to the director appear in italics.

Contents

- Sample Cover Letter
- Sample Calendar
- Center Policies and Procedures
- Expectations of Staff
- Program for Children
- Child Management

Sample Cover Letter

Welcome, staff of _____. We hope you will find much satisfaction in your work and discover many opportunities for professional growth during this new school year.

We have prepared this manual with the real understanding that it is classroom staff who make a program come alive. It is through the physical touch of a caring, knowledgeable, and sensible adult that children discover their unique place in their expanding world.

We hope you will spend time seriously studying these materials, especially the section on policies and procedures. This ensures school-wide uniformity in the approach to steady, wholesome growth and development.

Every time you call a family member, write an extra note, smile when you are tired, or attend a meeting, your effort will be appreciated and will maintain the quality of care we want at the center. Please take this broad outline of objectives and infuse it with your own special personality and talents.

Sincerely,

———————————————

Center Director

SAMPLE CALENDAR

August 21-27	Teacher Workshop (Parlor)
August 30	Family Orientation (Sanctuary and Rotunda Courtyard)
September 4	School Begins
October 8	Teachers In-service
October 16-18	School Pictures (Individual) (Room 108)
November 5	Parents Meeting (Rotunda, 7:30 p.m.)
November 6-7	Speech and Hearing Testing (Rooms 108 & 110)
November 12-16	Parent-Teacher Conferences
November 22-23	Thanksgiving Break
December 25-January 1	Holiday Break
January 2	School Resumes
January 24-25	Teachers In-service
February 1	Eye Tests
February 4	Parents Meeting (Rotunda, 7:30 p.m)
March 21	Teachers In-service
March 21	Open House and Book Fair
March 22	Book Fair
April 5-8	Spring Break
April 9 & 11	School Group Pictures
April 22	Parents Meeting (Rotunda, 7:30 p.m.)
May 15	Exhibit of Children's Art
June 15	Family-Staff Picnic (Playground Area, 1:00 p.m.)

CENTER POLICIES AND PROCEDURES

The list of statements below addresses policy questions frequently asked by families. A similar listing in your manual will help staff interact more effectively with families. It will also enhance your staff's feeling of being part of a well-informed team.

1. A nonrefundable check or cash for the registration fee must accompany enrollment forms.
2. A medical statement form (filled out by the child's physician and notarized) and a history of health information form (filled out by a family member or guardian) are provided by the center and should accompany all enrollment forms. Samples of these two forms are on pages 158-163. (See Appendix B for a sample letter on Health Tips.)
3. Enrollment for fall begins February 1 of the prior school year.
4. First month's tuition is due upon registration. This is nonrefundable in ordinary circumstances.
5. Families wishing to withdraw children must notify the school of this request in writing.
6. A required family orientation meeting is held before school begins to acquaint families with school policies and procedures and with the school program and teachers.
7. In emergency situations (such as severe weather or power failure) when area district schools are closed, we will also close until the situation is remedied.
8. Written reports of accidents are made by the director and filed with the bookkeeping department.

Safety Procedures

The following are some general classroom safety rules:
1. Children must not be left unsupervised at any time.
2. During arrivals and departures, a family member or carpool driver must accompany children to and from the classroom. During the school day, a teacher or aide must accompany children to special classrooms or the playground.
3. No hot drinks should be taken into the classroom except when the children are not present.

4. Any emergency situations (illness, accident, custody problems) should be reported immediately to the center director. The center director will notify families when it is appropriate to do so.

Fire Drill Procedures

The procedures for exiting the building in case of a fire are posted in a conspicuous place in the classroom. Teachers should be sure to inform any classroom assistant, student teacher, volunteer, or substitute concerning fire drills. A minimum of two fire drills a year will be held.

Teachers should study the fire evacuation route and practice with the children the first week or two of school. Anyone who smells smoke or suspects fire should pull the alarm.

Kindergarten and Nursery Groups. The aide leads children to the nearest exit, while the teacher checks the bathroom and classroom, takes the attendance book, and follows the group to a designated meeting place. The teacher takes attendance.

Toddlers. The assistant goes to the toddler room, and the aide and assistant take the children through the nearest exit door. The teacher checks the room and takes attendance at a designated meeting place.

Infants. All infants are placed in one crib, which is wheeled out the nearest exit door (in the toddler room) to a designated meeting place. The teacher checks the room and takes attendance at the meeting place.

Cafeteria. Children file out through kitchen exits or up ramps, depending upon the origin of fire, to the front entrance. The aide leads each group, and the teacher brings up the rear.

Nurse. The nurse takes any child in his or her office out the front door to the meeting place.

Director. The director checks all corridors and all bathrooms that are not in classrooms.

Playground Safety

Teachers are to position themselves in different parts of the playground areas so that they may observe all children and activities. Help the children learn and observe the following rules:

1. Do not run or walk behind or in front of swings.
2. No throwing of sticks, sand, rocks, and so on. (Please see that the children do not take sand from sand piles. Especially watch the drain area near the new little sand pile—if this fills with sand, you've got trouble!)
3. No running with sticks or other "harmful" objects.
4. No standing or jumping on picnic tables.
5. No climbing on fences.
6. "Space" yourself on slides and go up and come down without dawdling.
7. Do not take toys outside to the playground.

Teachers must remember that they are on the playground solely to supervise the children, not to do any other kind of work.

Field Trip Safety

Each child must bring in a written permission slip, which are filed by the teachers, before the first field trip is taken. The teacher should check these forms carefully before the first trip. Following are a few simple rules to adhere to:

1. Children must be loaded into cars at the curb side of the vehicle or under the carport.
2. Children must be secured in cars with seat belts. This is a must.
3. Children are to be accounted for before, during, and after field trips by roll call or head count. Each child should wear an identification tag with the name and telephone number of the center.
4. The teacher must give the director a note at the end of each field trip to let him or her know how many children and how many adults went, the date, and the place they visited. The director must keep this for insurance purposes and also for the director's records.
5. Classes of three-, four-, and five-year-olds are expected to take at least three field trips a year, more if desired by the Head Teacher. One adult to each three to five children is suggested, depending upon the age of the children.

Policy on Food

The center provides refreshments, but teachers are encouraged to be creative. Use a small portion of the classroom budget for extra treats from time to time, making sure that they are wholesome (for example, fruit, vegetables, cheese, crackers, and so on). Never feed the children popcorn, nuts, or anything small. These can easily be inhaled into the windpipe.

There are usually three or four holiday parties a year planned for each class. Parents usually plan and provide food (and games for older children). Birthdays can be celebrated very simply; try to limit these celebrations to treats the child can serve to the other children, such as cupcakes or cookies (no favors!).

Encourage the children to talk quietly when they are eating. Remember that a laughing child with food in his or her mouth can become a potentially dangerous situation.

Poisonous Plants

A list of poisonous plants is posted in various areas of the center. Be sure to inform yourself of these, and check the list before placing any plant in a classroom.

Policy on Toileting

When a child is in the process of being toilet trained, staff is expected to follow the procedures below in case of an "accident."

1. Quietly take the child to the bathroom.
2. Never leave the child alone in the bathroom.
3. Help the child into clean clothing.
4. Put soiled clothing into a plastic bag and put the bag in the child's tote.
5. Teach the child to wash his or her hands after using the toilet.
6. Do not be critical of the child, but be supportive and offer praise for positive behavior.

Expectations of Staff

Procedures for Record Keeping

Teachers should turn in all initial children's records to the assistant's office by the end of the first week of school. Teachers should report any incomplete or missing forms to the director. The medical release forms must be notarized before they are accepted by the center. Children's records should be kept in individualized folders in the assistant's office. These files should remain confidential and are kept locked at lunchtime and at the end of the day.

Classroom Management

1. Quietly take the child to the bathroom.
2. Never leave the child alone in the bathroom.
3. Help the child into clean clothing.
4. Put soiled clothing into a plastic bag and put the bag in the child's tote.
5. Teach the child to wash his or her hands after using the toilet
6. Do not be critical of the child; instead, be supportive and offer praise for positive behavior.

Equipment and Supplies

An allowance will be allocated annually for each classroom. It is the teacher's responsibility to keep his or her own record of expenditures and to budget the money to last the full year. Receipts must be presented for reimbursement. All invoices must be cleared with the director before the last day of school.

Filing and storage of teaching materials should be the responsibility of staff persons on a rotating basis. The following are some guidelines for using such materials:

1. All items are to be signed out.
2. Items must be returned within five days.
3. Items are to be returned to their proper place on the shelf in the supply room.

4. All books, games, puzzles, records, and so on should be complete when returned.

5. Be considerate of the needs of others when taking materials—do not deplete a category.

All maintenance requests should be handled through the center director. To report a maintenance problem, faculty may obtain forms in the assistant's office.

Teacher Attendance at Meetings

1. All teachers must attend teacher workshops.

2. Attendance at weekly staff meetings is required. The staff and director will determine the days and times. The purpose of staff meetings is threefold: to help each other with ideas, suggestions, approaches, and input regarding children; to create a bond among staff that will promote the same sense of community in classes; and to provide a forum for ideas from staff members (such a forum will improve service to the children and result in optimum job satisfaction and fulfillment for staff as professionals).

3. Teacher "visitation" day in the fall is set aside for each teacher to visit and observe in another center, preferably a class with the same age children as his or her own class.

4. Attendance at family meetings is expected of teachers and usually helps complete their required hours of training.

Responsibility to Families

1. Protect the health and safety of each child as a family would protect the child.

2. Learn as much about the family and home life as you can—it will be helpful in working with the child.

3. Be careful not to jump to any conclusions about a family's methods of training without knowing the facts.

4. Respect the privacy of families by overlooking any family secrets the child may divulge.

5. Respect the family's right to decide what is best for their child. When there is a direct conflict with school policy, explain the policy as tactfully as possible. If there is still disagreement, refer the matter to the director.

6. Know each child well enough to be able to give the family a reasonably accurate and concise verbal report when it is requested. Confine such reports to information about the child, taking care not to make comparisons or to give any information about other children in the group.

7. Establish a system for the care of clothing that will keep damage or loss to a minimum.

8. Call the family to report any incidents, falls, scratches, or unusual emotional experiences. This is in addition to the report that will be made out by the director. A call from the teacher reassures the family. A written report, prepared by the child's teacher, should be put in the child's folder.

Family-Teacher Conferences

Family-teacher conferences are of much value to the preschool teacher. By learning about the background and home environment of the child, the teacher is able to be more effective in working with the child. Always keep in mind that the goals of the family for the child are most important, and the school must work within this framework.

Before a conference is held, the teacher needs to prepare by doing a complete observation and evaluation of the child. Choose the area in which the child does best, being careful to bring this up early in the discussion with the family. Ask for suggestions from the family as to what the school can do for the family. Ask them if they have any questions about the program, policy, or schedule of the school. By this point in the conference, the teacher has the "feel" of the family, and hopefully trust has developed.

If there is a problem, it is best to wait and mention it after a rapport with the family has been established. Begin by asking if the problem has been noticed at home. Ask for suggestions from the family, being careful not to be judgmental or put the family on the defensive. Emphasize the point that the school works with the family. Be sure to have specific suggestions ready about solutions to the problem. If necessary, consult with others on the staff before the conference, and always inform the director when a conference with a family is scheduled. End the session by reaffirming the positive aspects of the conference and give the family an invitation to return at any time.

A written report should be placed in the child's folder. *The Family-Teacher Conference From on page 164 is a sample form to use in preparing such a report.*

Reports on Children

The director, program manager, and staff need to develop a style of report to use that best suits the needs of the center. A narrative style can be used for any age group.

Making daily observations, planning activities that will help you assess the level of skills, and having sensitive interactions with each child can form the basis for a comprehensive report on a child's progress. Give specific information rather than judgments. For instance, "Sam speaks clearly and with enthusiasm on a one-to-one basis with the teacher, but only occasionally is ready to share his ideas during group time." Writing a satisfactory report in a narrative style takes practice.

Once the teacher has collected the necessary information by anecdotal record keeping and other notes, he or she can use the following outline.

Name: [last, first]
Age: [years, months]
Date:
Teacher:

Start with a general description of the child (for example, size, weight, and what one notices first), then discuss the child's strengths as you perceive them. Use headings, as shown below, so that information can be found at a glance.

Outline for Report

Social
- How did the child initially adjust to the center and what progress has he or she made since then?
- Has he or she made friends? (Have names in case families want to build on these friendships.)
- Does he or she spend time alone? How much?
- Has he or she been excluded, rejected, or teased by others?

- What were the circumstances? How did the children or adults handle these situations?
- Can he or she empathize with others?
- In general, how does he or she get along with peers and with adults?
- What are the goals for social development in the next months?

Emotional

- Does he or she seem generally happy? Sad? Depressed?
- Does he or she like coming to the center? Does he or she seem happy early/later in the morning?
- Does he or she become involved in activities?
- How does he or she handle frustration (waiting a turn, aggressive feelings, and so on)?
- Is he or she able to verbalize?
- Does his or her mood change often? Fluctuate widely?
- Is he or she depending too much on adult support?
- How does he or she seem to feel about him- or herself?

Cognitive

- Does he or she seem to understand what you say?
- Can he or she make his or her wants known?
- Is he or she alert to what is going on around him or her?
- Can he or she initiate a project, plan, and follow through?
- Does he or she explore and experiment?
- Does he or she know shapes, colors, numbers, number concepts, and letters? Does the child read? At what level?
- Can he or she learn poems, songs? Follow rhythm?
- Can he or she do puzzles? How intricate?
- Does he or she know his or her name, address, phone number, and family member's names?

Physical

- Fine motor—cutting, sewing, building with small blocks
- Gross motor—balance, climbing, running, jumping, skipping
- Coordination—pouring juice, other similar activities
- Self-help (toilet, dressing skills, and so on)

Closing

- Goals for the future
- Reaffirm strengths

Staff Evaluations

The purpose of evaluation is to enhance performance. The process begins with identifying areas of strength and areas that need improvement. Evaluation is only one part of a broad process of professional development.

When the director visit the staff member's classroom for evaluating performance, he or she should observe the following areas:

Areas of Evaluation

Environment

- Is there a science center?
- Is it the kind of center that children can touch and through which they can learn?
- Does it evoke interest?
- Has the teacher planned it based on comments of a child in the group?

Cleanliness

- Are shelves and displays clean?
- Do they show order?
- Are they attractive to look at?
- Do children participate in cleaning up after each activity?
- Do they stack the blocks according to size and shape?
- Is there a comfortable place for the children when they arrive?
- Are the displays of children's work at children's eye level?

Atmosphere

- Is it warm and accepting?
- Is there a sense of order?

Activities

- Are the activities an integrated part of a long-range plan?
- Is there music every day?
- How often do children use rhythm instruments?
- If you see a child who lacks a skill, does the teacher include activities in her or his lesson plan to teach that skill?
- Does the teacher make daily notations?

- Is planning balanced in all areas: math, music, poetry, gross motor, drama, and so on?
- Does the teacher teach activities in various ways, such as tactile, verbal, and visual?

Classroom Management

- Is there a sense of order?
- Do the children know the routine?
- Do the children understand expectations?
- Do the staff and children demonstrate manners?
- Is the teacher monitoring each child's progress in the area of listening skills?
- Does the teacher maintain a specific schedule appropriate to the age group (see Sample Schedule on page 165) and adhere to it as closely as possible?

Aides

- Is the aide an integrated part of the group?
- Does the teacher invite the aide to take part in planning sessions and clearly explain his or her expectations?
- Do the adults and children treat the aide in a dignified manner?

Use of Available Materials and Resources

- Does the teacher make use of a wide range of equipment?
- Does the teacher visit the local library and other community resources?
- Is the teacher conscientious about the care and storage of materials?

Communication Skills

- Does the teacher channel questions, comments, areas of concern, and suggestions to the appropriate people?
- Does the teacher use the support staff and the director?
- Does the teacher make requests in writing?
- Does the teacher share materials and ideas, and give support to peers?
- Does the teacher clear all plans for family-teacher conferences with the director?

Program for Children

The objective is to create a context in which a meaningful program for children can flourish. For this, the center needs a philosophy of education and a plan for implementation. Much of this might be delegated to professional staff, or might be done by the director or together with staff.

Here for your review is the program guide prepared for a child care center. However, keep in mind that just reading through this material does not give a complete picture of what makes for a quality environment for young children.

First, there must be a genuine respect for the dignity of the children and an unconditional acceptance of them as they are. The preschool, more than anywhere else, is the place for individualized attention to develop children's curiosity, concern, and commitment to knowing—rather than the storing of facts.

There must be fluidity in the program and physical set-up, so that children can move about to the areas that fill their needs on a particular day. For example, it is interesting to watch children who are having problems with tensions and aggressions gravitate on their own to the water play or painting easels. It is important that water, play dough, and easels be readily available to the children.

A quality child care program does not rely on television. If television watching is permitted, it is limited to short intervals of time and to appropriate educational programs. Daily schedules include reading books and/or telling stories (story time) every day and preferably, several times a day. Story time provides quality literature that evokes the children's interest.

Music and movement activities are an equally important part of the program. Young children are developing and refining their motor abilities during the first six years of life. Children need to dance, play active games, run, climb, and learn to share space. Their listening skills are developing and becoming refined. They need to hear and experience a variety of tempos, rhythms, and types of music.

A problem noted in some centers is the lack of opportunity for the children to work (or not work) alone and to have the opportunity to plan and execute a project by themselves. This is not to deny the benefits of working cooperatively, but both situations should be available.

We want to emphasize the importance of a child sustaining a relationship with a primary caregiver. This is vital for the young child who is first moving out from the family nest. The teacher who is regular in attendance, warm in attitude, and fair and honest in his or her relationships with the children does much to foster in them a secure, happy attitude toward outside society.

Cognitive work has a definite place in the preschool/child care center, but without joy, security, and acceptance in the environment, it is of little value. This program is planned to enhance the development of skills and to strengthen feelings of empathy and community. Some instruction in science, math, reading readiness, and safety are included, as well as an enlargement of the child's world by telling them about other people and different customs. We want to provide a balanced and exciting day without destructive pressures.

Infants

The caregiver of infants is a person who enjoys "connecting" with the babies in his or her care. Good eye contact, talking and singing, holding, massaging, and rocking are all necessary interactions to help babies develop optimally.

Certainly we place the highest priority on attending to the physical needs of the infant, with careful attention given to hygiene. The caregiver must understand the signals given by each infant in expressing such needs as hunger or discomfort, and the need for stimulation. The caregiver also is aware that sensitive, consistent responses to the infant's needs will help foster a sense of trust between the child and teacher. This will become part of a foundation leading to healthy interactions with others throughout the child's life. The caregiver should complete The Infant Daily Report form (see page 166) for each child and show it to the family at the end of the day.

Needs of Infants

Feeding

1. Be sure to keep all food and formula refrigerated. Bacterial growth begins in a very short time when food is left at room temperature.
2. Keep accurate daily records of the kinds and amounts of food and drinks given to each child.
3. Feed babies their bottles by hand—do not prop bottles.
4. Wash your hands before and after you feed an infant.
5. Offer nutritious snacks.

Changing

1. Thoroughly wash and disinfect the changing area each day.
2. Be sure to use clean paper on the changing table each time you change a diaper.
3. Wash and dry the baby's bottom at each change.
4. Keep the baby secure, always keep your hands on him or her, and never leave the baby on a changing table or turn your back while he or she is on the table.
5. Use this occasion to talk and sing to the baby.
6. Wash your hands thoroughly after each diaper change.
7. Keep a daily record of bowel movements and diaper change times.

Sleep or rest

1. Change the crib sheets at the beginning of each day and as often as necessary during the day.
2. Put the child's name on the crib.
3. Be sure the crib is well spaced from the next crib, and has nothing in it that the child could climb on and thus fall out. Do not string toys across the crib.
4. As much as possible, rest time should be individualized. Infants vary in their need for sleep. Back rubbing is helpful for relaxing them. To minimize sudden infant death syndrome (SIDS), make sure babies sleep on their backs.
5. Record the time and length of naps on a daily chart.

Safety

Children at this age are very curious and are most likely to put *everything* in their mouths. For this reason, you must make absolutely sure that their play and sleep areas are free of any small objects that could be placed in mouths, noses, or ears.

1. Remove small button-like objects from stuffed animals.
2. Be sure there are no pebbles or stones on the floor.
3. Strings or threads that may be found on the edges of blankets and other items are very dangerous—a small child can choke on them.
4. Check other toys for small parts and remove them.
5. Check toys and play areas for sharp edges and report them.
6. Never leave drawers or doors open.

Special precautions must also be taken regarding electrical outlets and cords.
1. To a baby, an electrical outlet is a "wonderful place" because it has tiny holes that tiny fingers can fit into. For this reason, be sure each electrical outlet has safety caps on both sides.
2. Do not leave any electrical cords hanging within a baby's reach. Small appliances can fall and severely injure a baby.
3. Never touch an electrical cord or appliance while washing a baby.

The play area (creeping, crawling, and walking area) should be clean and bright, and offer stimulating learning experiences (new textures, shapes, sizes, colors, mirrors, mobiles, tunnels, rugs, and so on). Toys should be bright, unbreakable, washable, too big to swallow, and free of sharp edges.

Be close enough to the children to be able to protect them from hurting each other. Hair pulling and biting are common and natural behaviors. Be sure the infants who need to bite have clean, sanitized teething rings.

Practice evacuation of the building using a wheeled crib or similar equipment so babies will become accustomed to the routine.

Toddlers

Toddlers require extremely sensitive, secure teachers who have a well-developed sense of humor and plenty of physical stamina. Many people feel this is the most demanding department in the child care center. Perhaps this is because toddlers become frustrated so often during the day and need constant supervision given with a "light touch." These children do not have the language to explain their needs easily. If they want something, they take it. Although this makes sense when you understand their stage of development, it also creates problems in group living. Careful observations enable caregivers to know which situations lead to tantrums, most of which can then be prevented.

The beginning walker falls down a lot. Imagine how frustrated this can make a child feel. The child is becoming interested in pegs and blocks, but his or her fine motor skills are often not up to these tasks. They use their large muscles more often and to greater advantage; therefore, pull-toys and lifting exercises are really enjoyable. The caregiver needs to create a "child-centered" room with toys within the capabilities of the children and to tailor the schedule to meet their needs.

The toddler also likes music and being with other children. If the music and play become too boisterous, however, the toddler is apt to be overstimulated. Caregivers need to be aware that a drop in appetite is common in toddlers; therefore, they should offer food without making meals a "big deal." Even though they are becoming independent, toddlers like to know that their caregiver is nearby. They experience fears such as being in the dark, hearing loud thunder, changes in routine, and separation from family. Although they show warm affection for peers and adults, sharing with others is very difficult for them.

Add all these characteristics to the fact that toilet training is usually taking place, and it is no wonder that toddler caregivers need to be provided with the best support system possible. Always remember that the calendar is a poor measurement of a child's progress.

Caregivers can use the sample form, Goal Statement and Assessment for Toddlers, on pages 167-169 to record a toddler's skills and development in a number of areas. The forms can then be used as a source for planning future activities or as information for family-teacher conferences.

Three- and Four-Year-Olds

The major goal of the program for three- and four-year-olds is to build security for the child. Security leads to independence, which leads to exploration. This, in turn, leads to the development of skills. The classroom teacher of three- and four-year-olds needs to encourage independence and responsibility but remain available to children who suffer temporary setbacks and frustrations. Caregivers need positive self-esteem, because they are models for young children.

Young children acquire knowledge about the physical and social worlds in which they live by playful interaction with objects and people. Children are motivated by their desire to make sense of their world. The classroom needs to be filled with a variety of hands-on materials and games. A quality program should include:

1. Multiple experiences with language—read, speak, and listen to them, and sing with them
2. Informal number experience
3. Creative expression through music, art, and dance activities
4. Information at the children's level
5. Hands-on activities
6. Practice to develop and refine skills
7. Opportunity to build empathy with people
8. Opportunity for making choices

The child should have balance between:
1. Active and passive activities
2. Individual and group work
3. Emphasis on social, physical, emotional, aesthetic, and intellectual development
4. Indoor and outdoor activities

The teacher should observe and assess children a minimum of twice a year. Normally, late fall and late spring make the best assessment times. Use the Developmental Progress Report (pages 170-172) as a guide. The teacher can share this form with families during family-teacher conferences, or use it as an information item during such conferences. Every state has different requirements for the number of conferences to be held each year, so remember to correlate your family-teacher conferences with your local state requirements.

Child Management

The following was adapted from the University of Minnesota—Agricultural Extension Service Bulletin #321-6.

Disciplining means teaching children the rules people live by and directing them so they will adopt these rules of their own accord. Guiding children toward self-discipline is a goal you should keep in mind each day.

Discipline and punishment are not the same thing. The purpose of punishment is to prevent a child from repeating a forbidden act—to point out what is wrong. Punishment, however, is at the most a short-term deterrent. It is an ineffective way of educating children about rules and values. The purpose of discipline, on the other hand, is to direct a child in choosing constructive behavior patterns and in developing self-control and self-discipline.

Discipline implies a constructive viewpoint. The way you feel when you discipline children has a great effect on their reactions. For example, if you approach a behavior situation feeling cross, angry, and upset, the child will probably react in the same way. But if you are firm without being angry, the effect will be quite different. Let's examine several ways you can set the stage for discipline.

Suggest in a positive way. "Bounce the ball on the floor" is a positive suggestion. It tells children what to do. "Don't hit the window" is a negative one. It only tells children what not to do. Likewise, "Carry the glass of milk slowly" is a better way of saying, "Don't spill the milk." In other words, telling children what they should do is better than dwelling on what they shouldn't do.

It's very easy to let the words "Stop" and "Don't" slip out when you have to stop a child from doing something. It takes effort to replace those negatives with positive statements. But children will be less resistant if you make your suggestions positively, and you'll feel better about disciplining, too. Save "Don't" and "Stop" for those emergencies when you must put a quick stop to what is being done.

Let your tone of voice do part of the job. Certainly caregivers have plenty of cause for shouting at times, and who's to say it isn't a great release. But as a regular technique in disciplining children, shouting is not effective.

When are children most apt to listen to you? Is it when you speak loud and fast, or when you slow down and speak in a quiet, pleasant voice? If you speak in a loud tone of voice continually, the children probably will raise their voices to match yours.

It's better not to shout at young children from one room to another. When they play, children often concentrate so completely on what they are doing, that they are aware of nothing else. So move close and speak directly to them—you will be more apt to gain their attention. Not only is speaking quietly more effective in disciplining children, but it helps you stay calm, too.

Choose words that build confidence. Even though you must show disapproval when children misbehave, you can do it in a constructive way. You may feel like saying, "You naughty girl" or "You bad, bad boy," but such expressions belittle a child; they may make children feel guilty or lose confidence in themselves. It's better to show disapproval of what children are doing than disapproval of children themselves. To say, "Jimmy, keep your food on your plate" helps Jimmy more than "You naughty child—to make all that work for me."

Contrary to the way it may seem, children prefer to do what is expected of them and behave better when they sense love and approval. If through your disciplining you can say, "I don't like what you did, but I still love you," you'll be on the right track.

Keep your suggestions and directions to a minimum. Children tend to talk a lot. Though children need to be talked to, you need not fall into the habit of responding to everything they say. Also, offering too many suggestions to children can prevent them from using their own ideas. Making suggestions before children need help deprives them of the chance to work out their own problems and may upset their play.

Recommended Reading

Bronson, M.B. (2000). Recognizing and supporting the development of self-regulation in young children. *Young Children*, 55(2, March), 33-37.

Brazelton, T.B. (1994). *Touchpoints: Your child's emotional and behavioral development*. Cambridge, MA: Perseus Books.

Cartwright, S. (1999). What makes good preschool teachers? *Young Children*, 54(4, July), 4-7.

Da Ros, D.A. & B.A. Kovach. (1998). Assisting toddlers and caregivers during conflict resolutions: Interactions that promote socialization. *Childhood Education*, 75(1, Fall).

Dodge, D.T. & L.J. Colker. (1992). *The creative curriculum*. Washington, DC: Teaching Strategies.

Dombro, A.L., L.J. Colker, & D.T. Dodge. (1999). *The creative curriculum for infants and toddlers*. Washington, DC: Teaching Strategies.

Goleman, D. (1995). *Emotional intelligence*. New York: Bantam Books.

Haas-Foletta, K. & M. Cogley. (1990). *School-age ideas and activities for after school programs*. Nashville, TN: School Age Notes.

MacDonald, S. (1997). *Portfolio and its use: A road map for assessment*. Beltsville, MD: Gryphon House.

Schiller, P. (1996). *Practices in the early childhood classroom*. Columbus, Ohio: SRA.

Resources

ERIC/EECE
University of Illinois at Urbana-Champaign
Children's Research Center
51 Gerty Drive
Champaign, IL 61820-7469
(800) 583-4135
http://ericps.crc.uiuc.edu/ericeece.html

Day Care Forms Package
http://www.nationalchildcare.com/formspackage.htm

Complete with software to personalize and customize each form. Includes applications, financial agreements, health polices, parent policies, progress reports, past due account notices, accounting sheets, re-registration letters, sign-in sheets, transportations releases, dismissal forms, curriculum guidelines, and more.

National Resource Center for Health and Safety in Child Care
UCHSC at Fitzsimons
Campus Mail Stop F541
PO Box 6508
Aurora, CO 80045-0508
(800) 598-KIDS
http://nrc.uchsc.edu/

Curriculums

Albrecht, K. & L. Miller. *Innovations: The Comprehensive Infant Curriculum*. Beltsville, MD: Gryphon House.

Albrecht, K. & L. Miller. *Innovations: The Comprehensive Toddler Curriculum*. Beltsville, MD: Gryphon House.

Schiller, P., A.F. Ada, & C. Hurst. *The DLM Early Childhood Program*. Worthington, OH: SRA

Schiller, P. & K. Hastings (1998). *The Complete Resource Book*. Beltsville, MD: Gryphon House.

Sample Medical Statement

I give my permission to (child's physician) to complete this form with any information that would be useful for the planning of a program for my child.

Parent's signature: _____

Child's name: _____ Date of Birth: _____

Address: _____

Telephone: (_____) _____ Date of last examination: _____

PHYSICAL EXAM:

Weight _____   Height _____   Blood pressure _____

Heart _____   Chest _____   Throat _____

Abdomen _____   Genitourinary _____   Skin _____

Extremities _____   Vision _____   Hearing results _____

HBG _____   HCT _____   Urine _____

Lead test results: _____

PHYSICAL CHARACTERISTICS:

Color of eyes _____

Color of hair _____

Any identifying marks _____

IMMUNIZATIONS – (DATES):

D.P.T.   SABIN   TINE

Measles

Mumps

Rubella

Check if the child has had any of the following and indicate dates:

- ☐ Accidents
- ☐ Allergies
- ☐ Ear infections
- ☐ Strep throat
- ☐ Scarlet fever
- ☐ Seizures
- ☐ Rheumatic fever
- ☐ Asthma
- ☐ Bronchitis
- ☐ Heart disease
- ☐ T.B.
- ☐ Diabetes
- ☐ Poliomyelitis
- ☐ Tonsillitis
- ☐ Chicken pox
- ☐ Measles
- ☐ Mumps
- ☐ Kidney disease
- ☐ Operations
- ☐ Orthopedic treatment
- ☐ German measles
- ☐ Rubella
- ☐ Diphtheria
- ☐ Whooping cough
- ☐ Polio
- ☐ Other _____

Does the child have any congenital anomaly? If so, explain.

_____

Does the child take any medication regularly?

_____

Will the child require administration of any medications while at the center? If so, which one(s) and for what reason(s)? Also, do you offer any suggestions to staff for the administration of the medication?

_____

Has the child ever been hospitalized? If so, please explain. Give date(s) and reason(s).

_____

If relevant to planning a program for the child, please comment on the hospitalization.

_____

Does the child have any language or speech problems?

_____

Has the child's growth development been normal?

_____

List any physical/emotional conditions that would affect the child's participation in a child care program.

_____

Are there any restrictions/limitations on the child's participation in the program?

_____

Physician: _____ Date: _____

Notary: _____ Date: _____

_____

Health Information and Developmental History

Child's name: _____ Birth date: _____
                      Last, First   Day, Month, Year

HEALTH INFORMATION

Doctor's Name _____

Address _____

Phone # _____

What communicable disease has the child had? ☐ Measles (Big Red) ☐ Mumps

☐ Chicken Pox ☐ Whooping cough ☐ Measles (3 day) ☐ Other

Any serious illness or hospitalization? _____

Hospital preferred _____

Any physical disabilities? _____

Any known allergies other than food (asthma, hay fever, insect bites, others)?

_____

How many colds has your child had this past year?_____

How does the child react to an elevated temperature? _____

How does the child react to being ill? _____

Are any medications given regularly? _____

Has the child's doctor ever prescribed aspirin? _____

Are bowel movements regular? _____ How many a day? _____

What time(s)? _____

Is diarrhea or constipation a problem? _____

Any history of colic? _____

Is the baby's skin highly sensitive? _____

Frequent diaper rash? _____ Do you use: Oil? _____ Powder? _____

Lotion? _____ Other? _____

Are plastic pants used? ☐ Always ☐ Sometimes ☐ Never

Describe your child as you see him/her (appearance, personality, abilities).

_____

PERSONAL HISTORY

Child's Nickname _____ Place of Birth _____

Address _____

Language spoken at home (other than English) _____

Names and ages of siblings _____

Primary caretaker of child _____

Previous child care arrangements _____

Child's reaction to these arrangements _____

Does the child have a "fussy" time? _____ When? _____

How is it handled? _____

EATING:

Is the child usually hungry at mealtimes? _____ Between meals? _____

What are his/her favorite foods? _____

What foods are refused? _____

What eating problems does the child have? _____

Any food allergies? _____

Special feeding instructions _____

A.M. _____

P.M. _____

How has the child been fed? ☐ Lap ☐ High chair ☐ Other _____

TOILET HABITS: Toddler

Can the child be relied upon to indicate bathroom needs? _____

What word is used for urination? _____ For bowel movements? _____

Does the child need to go more frequently than usual for his/her age? _____

Is the child frightened of the bathroom? _____

Does he/she have accidents? _____

How does he/she react to them? _____

Was the child easy or difficult to train? _____

Does the child wet his/her bed at night? _____ How often? _____

Does the child use a potty chair, toilet, or toilet seat at home? _____

TOILET HABITS: Infant

Has toilet training been attempted? _____

What is used at home?

☐ Potty Chair ☐ Special toilet seat ☐ Regular toilet seat

SLEEPING:

What time does the child go to bed? _____ Awaken? _____

Is he/she ready for sleep? _____

Does he/she have own room? _____ Own bed? _____

Does he/she walk, talk, or cry out at night? _____

What does the child take to bed with him/her? _____

What is his/her mood upon awakening? _____

Does he/she take naps? _____ From _____ to _____

Do you have a special way to help the child go to sleep?

_____

SOCIAL RELATIONSHIPS:

Has he/she had experiences in playing with other children? _____

By nature is he/she ☐ friendly? ☐ Aggressive? ☐ Shy? ☐ Withdrawn?

How does he/she get along with brothers and sisters? _____

_____ Other adults? _____

With what age child does he/she prefer to play? _____

Does he/she know any children in the center? _____

Do you feel he/she will adjust easily to the child care situation? _____

_____

How does he/she relate to strangers? _____

Does he/she demand a lot of adult attention? _____

Does he/she enjoy being alone? _____

What makes him/her mad or upset? _____

How does the child show his/her feelings? _____

What do you find is the best way of handling him/her? _____

Who does most of the disciplining? _____

Is he/she frightened by: ☐ Animals?   ☐ Tall people?   ☐ Rough children?

☐ Loud noises?   ☐ Dark?   ☐ Storms?   ☐ Other? _____

Favorite toys and activities at home _____

Does he or she like to be read to? _____ Listen to music? _____

Does he or she prefer to play outdoors? _____

Can he/she ride a tricycle? _____

Has he/she had experience with: ☐ Clay?   ☐ Scissors? ☐ Easel Painting?

☐ Finger Painting?   ☐ Blocks?   ☐ Water Play?

COMMENTS

In what particular ways can we help your child this year? _____

How do you feel about child care for your child? _____

Will you be able to participate in your child's program? _____

What would you like to see us provide for your child? _____

Is there anything else we need to know in order to take better care of your child?

_____

Arrangements made for your child's care during illness are:

_____

_____   _____
(Parent's Signature)   (Date)

_____   _____
(Parent's Signature)   (Date)

Family-Teacher Conference

Name of Child _____ Age _____

Date of Conference _____ Class _____

Teacher _____

Teacher's Report and Comments _____

_____

_____

_____

_____

_____

_____

_____

_____

_____

_____

_____

_____

_____

Family's Comments and Response _____

_____

_____

_____

_____

(Use reverse side if necessary)

7:00	to	9:00	Greet the children, breakfast, free play
9:00	to	9:30	Circle time
9:30	to	11:00	Activities, snack at 10:15
11:00	to	11:30	Outside play or large motor play inside
11:30	to	11:45	Wash up, prepare for lunch, wash and set tables
11:45	to	12:30	Lunch
12:30	to	1:00	Story or records, cots
1:00	to	2:30	Nap time
2:30	to	3:00	Wake up, put cots away, have snack
3:00	to	3:30	Outdoor play
3:30	to	5:00	Activities, circle time, and free play
5:30	to	6:00	Clean up

Sample Schedule

Infant Daily Report

Child's name: _____ Date: _____

Caregiver: _____

Naps: **Additional comments:**

When? _____   _____

How Long? _____   _____

Bottles:

When? _____

What? _____

How Much? _____

Morning snack:

When? _____

What? _____

How Much? _____

Lunch:

When? _____

What? _____

How Much? _____

Afternoon snack:

When? _____

What? _____

How Much? _____

Diaper changes:

BM's _____

Goal Statement and Assessment for Toddlers

Name of Child _____

Date of Birth _____ Age _____

Department _____ Today's Date _____

Teacher _____

GROSS MOTOR ABILITIES:

A. Initial Movement
1. Moves total body with grace
2. Moves body parts independently of each other
3. Raises head
4. Directs hands toward a focal point
5. Directs feet to a focal point
6. Rolls over

B. Pretoddler Movement
1. Slides in any direction
2. Crawls
3. Sits alone
4. Stands
5. Bounces while sitting and standing
6. Kneels
7. Squats (stoop)
8. Stretches body
9. Climbs
10. Kicks
11. Twists body

C. Locomotor Skills
1. Walks
2. Runs
3. Jumps
4. Walks up and down stairs
5. Hops
6. Dances or jigs
7. Marches

D. Utilize the Body
1. Holds
2. Pulls
3. Pushes
4. Manipulates
5. Pours
6. Empties and fills
7. Stacks
8. Builds

Fine Motor Skills:

A. Initial Coordination
1. Grasps
2. Shakes
3. Points
4. Drops
5. Dangles
6. Bangs and pounds (taps)

C. Advanced Coordination
1. Scribbles
2. Turns pages
3. Picks and peels
4. Throws
5. Catches
6. Paints
7. Colors
8. Cuts
9. Handles eating utensils

Fine Motor Skills: Continued

B. Intermediate Coordination

1. Pulls
2. Assembles
3. Stirs
4. Squeezes
5. Rolls
6. Turns
7. Colors
8. Cuts
9. Handles eating utensils
10. Zips
11. Buttons
12. Laces
13. Ties

Cognitive Development:

A. Elementary Skills

1. Receives
2. Attends
3. Responds to stimulus
4. Imitates
5. Explores
6. Plays

B. Intermediate Skills

1. Matches and pattern
2. Recognizes familiar things and persons
3. Discriminates and sorts
4. Remembers
5. Locates
6. Persists

C. Advanced Skills

1. Follows directions
2. Solves problems
3. Initiates activities
4. Responds to simple sounds

Language Development:

A. Receptive Skills

1. Responds to sounds and locates its direction
2. Responds to own name
3. Identifies simple sounds
4. Responds to voices of various persons
5. Listens to short stories and looks at picture books

B. Production Skills

1. Babbles and chatters
2. Repeats sounds
3. Repeats single words and phrases
4. Repeats sentences
5. Initiates single words and phrases
6. Uses simple sentences
7. Recites simple nursery rhymes and fingerplays
8. Generates simple sentences
9. Speaks clearly

C. Applicable Skills

1. Follows simple directions
2. Asks questions
3. Makes requests for needs
4. Answers simple questions
5. Sings simple songs
6. Initiates conversation

PERSONAL AND SOCIAL DEVELOPMENT

A. Personal Management Skills

1. Picks up objects when he or she drops them
2. Feeds him- or herself
3. Plays with simple toys
4. Dresses and undresses him- or herself
5. Manages toileting activities
6. Performs simple housekeeping chores
7. Manipulates simple toys and equipment
8. Cares for possessions
9. Plays alone

B. Interpersonal Relationships Skills

1. Works and plays alongside other children
2. Shares toys and equipment with other children
3. Assists others with simple tasks
4. Recognizes other children by name
5. Accepts help and suggestions when appropriate
6. Takes "turns" with other children
7. Exhibits concern for the difficulties of others
8. Shares adult attention with other children
9. Participates in group activities
10. Accepts share of responsibility without being told

C. Self-Appreciation Skills

1. Recognizes own picture or mirror image
2. Knows simple body parts
3. Expresses affection and responds to others
4. Exhibits an appropriate amount of security

Comments _____

_____

Teacher: _____ Date: _____

Developmental Progress Report

Child's name: _____ Date: _____

Teacher: _____ Date: _____

Language: Vocabulary

Names familiar objects in environment

Names an object by hearing its description

Identifies body parts

Demonstrates an understanding of relationships (same/different, up/down, top/bottom)

Uses descriptive words

Language: Communication

Tells own name

Expresses needs

Converses with peers

Participates in discussions

Describes a picture or piece of artwork

Uses complete sentences

Relates a story or experience in sequence

Uses plurals correctly

Gives appropriate answers to questions (for example, "What do you do when you are thirsty?")

Speaks clearly

Listening:

Answers to own name

Follows directions (three or more steps)

Listens to a story

Comprehends main idea of a story

Memory:

Adapts to classroom routine

Calls five peers by name

Repeats songs or poems with motions

Repeats digits in a given order (two or three)

Motor Coordination: Gross

Walks in a straight line

Runs in a designated path

Jumps in place

Balances on one foot

Throws a ball or bean bag into a can three feet away
Uses a hammer
Climbs stairs using alternating feet
Imitates simple rhythmic patterns
Claps to a given beat
Kicks a ball

Motor Coordination: Fine
Puts on a coat or sweater
Dresses self
Folds a piece of paper in half
Uses a pencil or crayon
Pastes
Holds scissors properly
Zips and buttons
Copies basic geometric shapes
Pours from a pitcher
Washes and dries hands
Builds a bridge using blocks
Draws a fairly recognizable human picture
Shows preference for dominant hand usage

Visual Discrimination: Objects
Recognizes similarities in objects
Recognizes differences in objects (sorting)
Matches similar shapes
Tells what is missing in incomplete pictures

Visual Discrimination: Colors
Matches like colors
Names colors

Visual Discrimination: Letters
Recognizes own name in print
Recognizes most letters in the alphabet

Auditory Discrimination:
Recognizes familiar sounds
Labels sounds as loud and soft
Reproduces a familiar sound
Identifies a familiar speaker

Social Development:

Plays/works well with others

Has made friends in school

Is happy

Adjusts easily to new situations

Work Habits:

Follows directions

Has appropriate attention span

Cleans up after work period

Values own work

Is observant

Is curious

Reaction to Teacher in School:

Demands teacher's attention

Seeks support of teacher before engaging in activity

Seeks constant step-by-step reinforcement while engaging in activity

Hesitates to interact with teacher in any way

Operates independently, but seeks help and support from teacher when necessary

Reaction to Directed Small Group Activity in the Classroom:

Disruptive

Silliness

Self-confidence—willing to follow

Withdrawal and no interaction with peers

Shyness

Approach to Problem:

Hesitates to attempt task on own

Eager to participate

Gives up easily

Solves problems on own

Able to organize

Needs to be shown task and supported

Does task after being shown how

Looks for constant approval

Shows confidence in ability to perform a task

Refuses to perform a task

Reaction to Free Choice of Activity:

Initiates activity on own

Uses a variety of materials

Uses same material in a variety of ways

Unable to make choice, wanders around the room aimlessly

Chooses the same activity every day

Stays with the activity until able to do something with it

Gets activity out and then leaves it

Interested more in process than end product

Chooses only activities in which the end product can be taken home

Socialization within the Room:

Only with the teacher

Special friend

No one

Freely with individuals in small groups

Awareness of Peers:

Talking

Showing an object

Touching

Kicking or pushing

Other

Attitude Toward Adults:

Affectionate

Trusting

Fearful

Angry

Other

Interaction with a Small Group:

Solitary play

Parallel play alongside, but not actually engaged

Cooperative play

Resources

Books

Adams, M. (1990). *Beginning to read*. Cambridge, MA: MIT Press.

Adams, M.J., B.R. Foorman, I. Lundberg, & T. Beeler. (1997). *Phonemic awareness in young children: A classroom curriculum*. Baltimore: Paul H. Brookes Publishers.

Albrecht, K. & L. Miller. (2000). *Innovations*: *The comprehensive infant curriculum*. Beltsville, MD: Gryphon House.

Albrecht, K. & L. Miller. (2000). *Innovations: The comprehensive toddler curriculum*. Beltsville, MD: Gryphon House.

Alexander, N. (2000). *Workshops that work!* Beltsville, MD: Gryphon House.

Armstrong, A. & C. Casement. (2000). *The child and the machine*. Beltsville, MD: Robins Lane Press.

Aronson, S., S. Bradley, S. Louchheim, D. Mancuso, and E. Unguary. (1997). *Model child care health policies*. Washington, DC: National Association for the Education of Young Children (NAEYC).

Baldwin, S. (1996). *Lifesavers: Tips for success and sanity for early childhood managers*. St. Paul, MN: Redleaf Press.

Brazelton, T.B. & S.I. Greenspan. (2000). *The irreducible needs of children: What every child must have to grow, learn, and flourish*. Cambridge, MA: Perseus Books.

Brazelton, T.B. (1994). *Touchpoints: Your child's emotional and behavioral development*. Cambridge, MA: Perseus Books.

Brazleton, T.B. (1992). *To listen to a child: Understanding the normal problems of growing up*. Cambridge, MA: Perseus Books.

Bruner, J. (1968). *Processes of cognitive growth: Infancy*. Worcester, MA: Clark University Press.

Burns, M.S., P. Griffin, & C.E. Snow, Eds. (1999). *Starting out right: A guide to promoting children's reading success*. Washington, DC: National Academy Press.

Cherry, C., B. Harkness, & K. Kuzma. (1987). *Nursery school and day care management*. Torrance, CA: Lake Publishing Group.

Collins, J.C. & J.I. Porras. (1997). *Built to last: Successful habits of visionary companies*. New York: Harper Business.

Couchenour, D. & K. Chrisman. (1999). *Families, schools, and communication: Working together for young children*. Albany, NY: Delmar Publishing Company.

Covey, S.R. (1989). *The 7 habits of highly effective people*. New York: Simon & Schuster, Inc.

Dodge, D.T. & L.J. Colker. (1992). *The creative curriculum*. Washington, DC: Teaching Strategies.

Dombro, A.L., L.J. Colker, & D.T. Dodge. (1999). *The creative curriculum for infants and toddlers*. Washington, DC: Teaching Strategies.

Elkind, D. (1988). *Miseducation: Preschoolers at risk*. New York: Knopf.

Elkind, D. (1998). *Reinventing childhood: Raising and educating children in a changing world*. Rosemont, NJ: Modern Learning Press.

Erickson, E. (1964). *Childhood and society*. New York: Norton.

Feeney, S. & N.K. Freeman. (1999). *Ethics and the early childhood educator: Using the NAEYC code*. Washington, DC: National Association for the Education of Young Children (NAEYC).

Fraiberg, S.H. (1996). *The magic years: Understanding and handling the problems of early childhood*. New York: Fireside.

Frost, J. (1992). *Play and playscapes*. Albany, New York: Delmar Publishing Company.

Gardner, H. (1983). *Frames of mind*. New York: Basic Books.

Goleman, D. (1995). *Emotional intelligence*. New York: Bantam Books.

Gordon, T. (1986). *Leader effectiveness training, L.E.T: The no-lose way to the productive potential of people*. New York: Bantam.

Graft, R. (1990*). Preschool director's survival guide: 135 forms, checklists, letters, and guidelines for day-to-day management*. Upper Saddle River, NJ: Prentice Hall Trade.

Haas-Foletta, K. & M. Cogley. (1990). *School age ideas and activities for after school programs*. Nashville, TN: School Age Notes.

Hannaford, C. (1995). *Smart moves: Why learning is not all in your head*. Arlington, VA: Great Ocean Publishers.

Healy, J.M. (1987). *Your child's growing mind: A guide to learning and brain development from birth to adolescence*. New York: Doubleday.

Hymes, J.L. (1981). *Teaching the child under six* (3rd ed.). New York: Merrill.

Katz, L. & D.E. McClellan. (1997). *Fostering children's social competence: The teacher's role*. Washington, DC: National Association for the Education of Young Children (NAEYC).

Kotter, J.P. (1999). *What leaders really do*. Boston, MA: Harvard Business School.

Lowe, P. (1995). *Creativity and problem solving: Complete training package*. New York: McGraw-Hill Companies.

McGraw, P. (1999). *Life strategies: Doing what works, doing what matters*. New York: Hyperion.

MacDonald, S. (1997). *Portfolio and its use: A road map for assessment*. Beltsville, MD: Gryphon House.

Miller, E.E. (1997). *The 10-minute stress manager* {audio cassette}. Carlsbad, CA: Hay House, Inc.

Montanari, E.O. (1992). *101 ways to build enrollment in your early childhood program*. St. Paul, MN: Redleaf Press.

Neuman, S., C. Copple, & S. Bredekamp. (2000). *Learning to read and write: Developmentally appropriate practices for young children*. Washington, DC: National Association for the Education of Young Children (NAEYC).

Neugebauer, R. & B. Neugebauer. (1998). *The art of leadership: Managing early childhood organizations*. Redmond, WA: Exchange Press.

Peters, T. & N. Austin. (1989). *A passion for excellence*. New York: Warner Books.

Peters, T. (1994). *The pursuit of WOW!* New York: Vintage Books.

Ramey, C.T. & S.L. Ramey. (1999). *Right from birth*. New York: Goddard Press.

Rubin, M., P. Frahm, & P. Frahm. (1993). *60 ways to relieve stress in 60 seconds*. New York: Workman Publishing Company.

Satter, E. (2000). *Child of Mine: Feeding with love and good sense*. Palo Alto, CA: Bull Publishing Company.

Schickedanz, J.A. (1999). *Much more than the ABC's: The early stages of reading and writing*. Washington, DC: National Association for the Education of Young Children (NAEYC).

Schiller, P. (1999). *Start smart: Building brain power in the early years*. Beltsville, MD: Gryphon House.

Schiller, P. & T. Bryant. (1998). *The values book*. Beltsville, MD: Gryphon House.

Schiller, P. (1998). *The complete resource book: An early childhood curriculum with over 2000 activities and ideas!* Beltsville, MD: Gryphon House.

Sciarra, J. & A.G. Dorsey. (1998). *Developing and administering a child care center* (3rd ed.). New York: Delmar Publishers.

Silberg, J. (2000). *125 Brain games for toddlers and twos*. Beltsville, MD: Gryphon House.

Silberg, J. (1993). *Games to play with babies*. Beltsville, MD: Gryphon House.

Silberg, J. (1993). *Games to play with toddlers*. Beltsville, MD: Gryphon House.

Sousa, D. (2000). *How the brain learns: A classroom teacher's guide* (2nd ed.). Thousand Oaks, CA: Families and Work Institute.

Sylwester, R. (1995). *A celebration of neurons: An educator's guide to the human brain*. Alexandria, VA: ASCD.

Taylor, B. (1996). *Early childhood program management: People and procedures*. Upper Saddle River, NJ: Prentice Hall.

Internet Resources

Children, Youth and Families Education and Research Network (CyferNet)
URL http://www.cyfernet.org
Links to professional organizations, electronic mail groups, and program management resources.

Child Care Online
URL http://childcare.net
Pruissen, C. (1999). *Caregiver aids: Business forms for caregivers & parents.*
Forms to calculate attendance, payment, and monthly income and expenses; weekly activity and menu charts; personal child and family files; accident reports; medication records; program planning schedules; and so on. Can be ordered online.

Daycare forms package: A collection of the most commonly used forms in child care (with software)
URL http://www.nationalchildcare.com/formspackage.htm

ERIC Educational Resources Information Center and ERIC/EECE Clearinghouse on Elementary and Early Childhood Education
URL http://www.ericeece.org
A national information system supported by the U.S. Department of Education. Database with search, publications on child care quality, LISTSERV discussion groups, resource lists, and conference calendar.

National Association for the Education of Young Children (NAEYC)
URL http://naeyc.org
Professional development, accreditation, conferences, publications, membership, journal *Young Children* with searchable index, and scholarly journal *Early Childhood Research Quarterly* with "Practitioners Perspectives." Online catalog of books, videotapes, brochures, and other resources.

National Child Care Information Center (NCCIC)
URL http://www.nccic.org
Large body of resources on quality child care.

National Network for Child Care (NNCC)
URL. http://nncc.org
This site aims to "make quality research, resources, and best practices available nationally for local access." Articles, assistance from child care experts, state

licensing information and statistics, discussion forum, and conference listings. Sponsored by the Cooperative State Research, Education, and Extension Service and the U.S. Department of Agriculture.

National Resource Center for Health and Safety in Child Care
URL http://www.nrc.uchsc.edu
Child care links from A to Z. Links to individual states' child care licensure regulations, and national health and safety performance standards.

Owners, Directors and Childcare Professionals Internet tools
URL http://www.watchmegrow.com/wmgdirector.htm

Reviews of small business accounting software (QuickBooks, Peachtree, MYOB, and so on) can be found at:
URL http://www.zdnet.com/products/stories/reviews/0,4161,2433824,00.html

Software Providers: a number of software providers offer information on child care centers and information management software (record keeping, child and family information, health forms, reports, permission forms, contracts, and so on). Some examples can be found at: URL
http://www.on-qsofttware.com, http://www.childcareadmin.com, http://www.providerware.com, http://www.sba.gov/library/pubs/mp-30.doc, http://www.daycaresoftware.com, http://www.kasksoftware.com, http://www.daycareorganizer.com

U.S. Small Business Administration (SBA). (1999). *Child day-care services.* Management and Planning Series Publication MP-30. Business plan, cash flow analysis, financial sources, marketing, operations models, appendices on state regulatory agencies, licensing, and information resources.
URL http://www.sba.gov/library/pubs/mp-30.doc

U.S. Small Business Administration (SBA). (1999). *How to Start a Quality Child Care Business.* Management and Planning Series Publication MP-29.
URL http://www.sba.gov/library/pubs/mp-29.doc

Viewing Systems for Child Care
URL http://www.parent-view.com, www.kinderview.com

Journals

Bronson, M.B. (2000). Recognizing and supporting the development of self-regulation in young children. *Young Children*, 55(2, March) 33-37.

Cartwright, S. (1999). What makes good preschool teachers? *Young Children*, 54(4, July), 4-7.

Da Ros, D.A. & B.A. Kovach. (1998). Assisting toddlers and caregivers during conflict resolutions: Interactions that promote socialization. *Childhood Education*, 75(1, Fall), 1-30.

Elswood, R. (1999). Really including diversity in early childhood classrooms. *Young Children*, 54(4, July).

Kupetz, B. (1998). "Do you see what I see?" Appreciating diversity in early childhood settings. *Early Childhood News*, (July/August).

Mogharreban, C. & S. Branscum. (2000). Educare: Community collaboration for school readiness. *Dimensions of Early Childhood*, 28(1, Winter).

Sussna, A.G. (2000). A quest to ban cute—and make learning truly challenging. *Dimensions of Early Childhood*, 28(2, Spring).

Tabors, P.O. (1998). What early childhood educators need to know. Developing effective programs for linguistically and culturally diverse children and families. *Young Children*, 53(6, November).

Magazines

Godt, P. (1999). Books can spark multicultural awareness. *Children and Families*, (Spring).

Gonzalez-Mena, J. & A. Stonehouse. (2000). High-maintenance parents. *Child Care Information Exchange*, (January/February).

Kostelnik, M.J. (1993). Recognizing the essentials of developmentally appropriate practice. *Child Care Information Exchange*, (March/April).

Schiller, P. (2000). A director's game plan. *Child Care Information Exchange*, (July/August).

Schiller, P. (1999). Turning knowledge into practice. *Child Care Information Exchange*, (March/April).

Schiller, P. (1998). The thinking brain. *Child Care Information Exchange*, (May/June). (order #12149)

Schiller, P. (1997). Brain development research: Support and challenges. *Child Care Information Exchange*, (September/October).

Wardle, F. (2000). Supporting constructive play in the wild: Guidelines for learning outdoors. *Child Care Information Exchange*, (May/June).

Your child: From birth to three. (1997). *Newsweek*. Special Edition, (Spring/Summer).

Your child: From birth to three. (2000). *Newsweek*. Special Edition, (Fall/Winter).

Organizations

I Am Your Child Campaign
335 North Maple Drive, Suite 135
Beverly Hills, CA 90210
(310) 285-2385
http://www.iamyourchild.org

Child Care Action Campaign
330 Seventh Avenue, 17th Floor
New York, NY 10001
(212) 239-0138

Children's Defense Fund
25 E. Street, NW
Washington, DC 20001
(202) 628-8787
http://www.tmn.com/cdf/index.html

Center for Career Development in Early Care and Education, Wheelock College
200 The Riverway
Boston, MA 02215
(617) 734-5200
http://ericps.crc.uiuc.edu/ccdece/ccdece.html

ERIC/EECE
University of Illinois at Urbana-Champaign
Children's Research Center
51 Gerty Drive
Champaign, IL 61820-7469
(800) 583-4135
http://ericps.crc.uiuc.edu/ericeece.html

Families and Work Institute
330 Seventh Avenue, 14th Floor
New York, NY 10001
(212) 465-2044
http://www.familiesandworkinst.org

National Association for Childcare Management
1255 23rd Street, NW
Washington, DC 20037
(202) 659-5955

National Association for the Education of Young Children (NAEYC)
1834 Connecticut Avenue, NW
Washington, DC 20009-6786
(800) 424-2460
Web: http://www.naeyc.org

National Association of Child Care Professionals (NACC)
304-A Roanoke Street
Christiansburg, VA 24063
(800) 537-1118
http://www.naccp.org
E-mail: admin@naccp.org

National Child Care Association (NCCA)
1029 Railroad Street
Conyers, GA 30207
(800) 543-7161
Web: http://nccanet.org
E-mail: nccallw@mindspring.com

National Head Start Association
1651 Prince Street
Alexandria, VA 22314
(703) 739-0875
http://www.nhsa.org

Resource for Childcare Management
P.O. Box 672
Bernardsville, NJ 07924
(202) 766-9237

Southern Early Childhood Association (SECA)
formerly Southern Association on Children Under Six
7107 West 12th Street, Suite 102
PO Box 56130
Little Rock, AR 72215-6130
(800) 305-SECA
Web: http://www.seca50.org

Zero to Three: National Center for Infants, Toddlers, and Families
734 15th Street, NW, Tenth Floor
Washington, DC 20005-2101
(202) 638-1144 or (800) 899-4301 for Publications
Web: http://www.zerotothree.org

Pamphlets and Reprints

Available from SECA (Southern Early Childhood Association)
7107 West 12th Street, Suite 102
PO Box 56130
Little Rock, AR 72215-6130
(800) 305-SECA
Web: http://www.seca50.org

Brochures
Moving and Playing
Childcare Checklist
Checklist for Diversity in Early Childhood Education and Care
Bright Ideas: Outdoor Play and Learning for Infants and Toddlers by Suzanne
    M. Winter (1995)
Caring for Infants and Toddlers with Special Needs by Staisey Hodge (1995)

Position Statements
Quality Child Care (1999)
Appropriate Use of Computers in the Early Childhood Curriculum (1999)
Developmentally Appropriate Assessment (1999)

Available from NAEYC (National Association for the Education of Young Children)
1834 Connecticut Avenue, NW
Washington, DC 20009-6786
(800) 424-2460
Web: http://www.naeyc.org

Position Statements
Developmentally Appropriate Practice in Early Childhood Programs
    Serving Infants (1989)
Developmentally Appropriate Practice in Early Childhood Programs Serving
    Toddlers (1989)
Developmentally Appropriate Practice in Early Childhood Programs Serving
    Young Preschoolers (1992)
Good Teaching Practices for Older Preschoolers and Kindergarteners (1994)

Available from Child Care Information Exchange
PO Box 3249
Redmond, WA 98073
(800) 221-2864

Article Reprints
Guide to Successful Fundraising, *Child Care Information Exchange*.
    Redmond, WA. Reprint #6
Marketing Your Child Care Program, *Child Care Information Exchange*.
    Redmond, WA. Reprint #4
Tools for Managing Your Center's Money, *Child Care Information Exchange*.
    Redmond, WA. Reprint #2.
Staff Selection, *Child Care Information Exchange*. Redmond, WA Reprint #7

Available from U.S. Consumer Product Safety Commission
Washington, DC 20207
(800) 638-2772 (hotline)
(301) 504-0051 (orders)
http://www.cpsc.gov

The Safe Nursery: A booklet to help avoid injuries from nursery furniture and
    equipment.
Child Care Safety Checklist for Parents and Child Care Providers

Index